MOM OVERBOARD

Robin Chaddock

Keep sailing!
Robin
Chaddock

HARVEST HOUSE PUBLISHERS

EUGENE, OREGON

Unless otherwise indicated, all Scripture quotations are taken from the HOLY BIBLE, NEW INTERNATIONAL VERSION®. NIV®. Copyright © 1973, 1978, 1984 by the International Bible Society. Used by permission of Zondervan. All rights reserved.

Verses marked THE MESSAGE are taken from The Message. Copyright © by Eugene H. Peterson 1993, 1994, 1995, 1996, 2000, 2001, 2002. Used by permission of NavPress Publishing Group.

Verses marked KJV are taken from the King James Version of the Bible.

Cover by Harvest House Publishers, Inc., Eugene, Oregon, Katie Brady, designer

Cover photo of mother and children © James Muldowney/Stone/Getty Images

Cover photo of swimming tube © Rubberball/Creatas

Harvest House Publishers and the author have made every effort to trace the ownership of all quotes. In the event of a question arising from the use of a quote, we regret any error made and will be pleased to make the necessary correction in future editions of this book.

MOM OVERBOARD
Copyright © 2004 by Robin Chaddock
Published by Harvest House Publishers
Eugene, Oregon 97402
www.harvesthousepublishers.com

Library of Congress Cataloging-in-Publication Data

Chaddock, Robin.
  Mom overboard / Robin Chaddock.
    p. cm.
Includes bibliographical references.
  ISBN 0-7369-1259-2 (pbk.)
  1. Mothers—Religious life. 2. Mothers—Conduct of life. I. Title.
  BV4529.18.C42 2004
  248.8'431—dc22   2003020631

All rights reserved. No part of this publication may be reproduced, stored in a retrieval system, or transmitted in any form or by any means—electronic, mechanical, digital, photocopy, recording, or any other—except for brief quotations in printed reviews, without the prior permission of the publisher.

Printed in the United States of America

04 05 06 07 08 09 10 11 / VP-KB/ 10 9 8 7 6 5 4 3 2 1

To my two kids, Madison and Grant—
two of the most entertaining, insightful, and delightful
creatures God ever made. Why God chose me to be
your mommy baffles me all the time,
but I'm glad he did!

Acknowledgments

I am deeply grateful to all of the remarkable mothers who made their contributions to this book. They were candid, real, and highly desirous of sharing their experiences of motherhood with other mothers. They offered their thoughts and understanding from the heart of a mother to the heart of other mothers.

From my remarkable circle of friends in Central Indiana, I want to thank Kathy Alderson, Karen Anders, Nancy Beasley, Celia Boeher, Beth Campbell, Susan Day, Donnae Dole, Carolyn Dorsey, Nancy Dresch, Linda Forler, Lynn Hartzell, Theresa Leibold, Susan Leichty, Jennifer Lipinski, Laura Lucas, Julie Pelton, Claudia Pierson, Michele Reel, Patti Riemersma, Libby Sandstrom, Sarah Tillbury, Ann Van Meter, Jill Zaniker, and the other mothers who wanted their names changed or withheld for personal reasons. You are all role models of mothering to me.

Another incredible community centers in the graduates of Christian Leaders, Authors and Speakers Services (CLASS). These professional writers and speakers generously shared their talents and insights, expecting nothing in return but my deep devotion and a free book. Thank you! They are Jennie Bishop, DenaRae Carlock, Sherry Cummings, Cheryl Jackubowski, Linda Kelly, Sally Philbrick, Ginger Plowman, Lori Scott, Diana Taylor, Diana Urban, Dawn Whitmore, Lori Wildenberg, Rhonda Wilson, Jeanne Zornes. To find out more about CLASS, please go to www.CLASSServices.com.

Two other authors who made wonderful contributions were Lynn Shaw, who let me use her signature story about the washing machine and the ABCs, and Celeste Lilly-Rossman, who continually inspires me with her poetic prose and obvious connection to our Creator.

Laurie Beth Jones has made invaluable contributions to my life and work by teaching me what it means to let God love me and work through me.

Terry Glaspey and Barbara Gordon of Harvest House were tremendously instrumental in the development of this book. Their keen eye for theme and structure, coupled with their deep passion for our readers, were inspirations to me as we made this into a book we hope will touch hearts and change lives for the glory of God.

My remarkable husband, David, is a constant source of steadiness, unconditional love, and unfailing belief in me and what I've been called to do. I know more about love through his example than I've ever known before.

Contents

Why Is Mommy Splashing Around?

When my son was four years old, he watched Disney's *Toy Story*. Grant was particularly taken by Buzz Lightyear, the intergalactic superhero whose signature phrase was "To Infinity and Beyond!"

One morning while both my children were young enough to be at home with me a large part of the day, I knew someone was going to go to time out in short order. As the consummate introvert, I was in need of a very large dose of quiet, and there was no quiet to be found. What I did have plenty of were toys on the floor, pudding cups littering the dining room table, spats to settle, and a television that was not playing what I wanted to be watching. I sat in the living room contemplating who should be sent to their room first, the kids or me.

Grant had been watching Buzz and wanted to imitate him, ready to save the galaxy. Running through the room with a makeshift cape tied to his shoulders, he shouted his own version of Buzz Lightyear's famous battle cry: "To Insanity and Beyond!"

I had no idea which to do first, howl with laughter or burst into tears. I was already living the insanity, so I wondered what could be in the beyond! Maybe I wanted to go there, maybe I didn't. But I knew I needed to be somewhere other than where I was. I realized at that point something I had suspected all along. I had been tossed from the mother ship, the S.S. Sanity. I was a mom overboard.

I soon discovered I wasn't the only mom splashing around. As I started to venture out and tell other mothers what I was experiencing, I realized many of us were feeling overscheduled and undervalued, overtired and undersupported. We expressed a sense of not knowing who we were anymore. In our everyday rush to meet everyone's needs, honor everyone's schedules, live up to everyone's expectations, and keep everyone happy, we felt thrown over the side of the identity boat. We were drowning.

And the pressures we moms feel extend beyond our internal desire to serve. There are powerful and compelling forces in society that pound on our ships and constantly threaten to capsize us. We can clearly identify cultural norms and expectations that keep us off balance.

The central message of this book is very clear, and I'm going to say it right out front: Unless you know who you are, why you're here, and what you're going to do with that information, you will be floundering, sinking, gasping for breath as a person, let alone as a mother. Unless you know, embrace, and act from your God-given identity, you will continually feel like a person overboard. This is especially important in the highly demanding and all-consuming role of motherhood. You will confidently sail through many troubled seas when you have and practice a keen understanding of your intimate relationship with God. He created you first of all to be in a loving relationship with him, and second, to fulfill a purpose he designed just for you.

This book offers you the Lifeboat of recovering your sense of identity. We'll also look at some wonderful little Lifesavers you can use every day to ensure that you are either swimming toward or staying onboard the sanity ship. You will be equipped to be spiritually strong and healthy, to walk wholeheartedly with Jesus, to have nourishing relationships, and to raise healthy kids.

Search and Rescue Tips

Becoming a sailing mom does not happen overnight. You need time for conversation, observation, and reflection. You need time alone and time in community.

The more you learn to recognize and implement the Divine Assignment Lifeboat and the Lifesavers, the more they become ingrained in you as you are transformed by God's Holy Spirit. You realize they are woven together in a special tapestry that is as beautiful as your favorite cotton throw or a newborn baby's heirloom blanket. Knowing your Divine Assignment frees you to laugh. Watching the unfolding in your children is cause to celebrate your family's uniqueness. Self-care and maintaining healthy connections are twin sisters.

It's very likely that you will want to keep a journal or guidebook while you are going through the "Search and Rescues," especially as you are writing your vision. When you are using this guide, keep a box of colored pencils, markers, or crayons close by. As you are moved by the Holy Spirit to add color to your journal or as you would like to illustrate in pictures something you are feeling or learning, you may want to reach for these art tools that are wonderful gifts from God. Likewise, keep a box of note cards on hand. You are sure to be reminded of mothers who inspire you and have influenced you in your quest of motherhood. Be generous in writing and sending notes along your way.

The "Search and Rescues" will be of no use to you unless you are ruthlessly truthful in your reflections and responses. As I learned from some very wise professors at one point in my career, you don't get A's for appearances. God calls us to faithfulness and integrity, not perfect success as defined by outward appearances. At the same time realize that you are on an archeological dig, excavating your true identity and call from God. Exercise the same care that archeologists use when they are searching for treasure to uncover and honor. They don't use arsenals of dynamite and sledgehammers to unearth their findings. They use tiny little scrapers and soft brushes to reveal little by little the beauty of their riches. You are brimming with riches yourself, so take the time and care needed so you don't damage anything in the process or miss any subtle artifact waiting to be discovered.

The discussion questions can be quite helpful to individuals. But I believe you will be even more richly blessed when you use them for group discovery. The lively, Spirit-filled exchange of people who are seeking God together produces a richness and depth to faith and revelation that cannot be found when one is dialoging with only oneself. So, I encourage you to gather and talk with other mothers to share what you have in common and how you are growing. The "Search and Rescue" questions at the end of each chapter will help you celebrate the unique perspectives and gifts you each have to offer. As you explore, you will be excited to let others know what you are discovering and how you are growing as a woman, mother, and partner of Christ.

For those of you involved in leading a group, there are additional suggestions at the end of this book.

You would be amazed at the number of mothers who, once they heard the title of this book, offered to pose for the cover. My prayer is there will be fewer and fewer takers as we learn how to expertly sail the sea of motherhood.

Part 1

You, Too, Can Sail!

1

The Plunge

Making the simple complicated is commonplace;
making the complicated simple, awesomely
simple, that's creativity.

—CHARLES MINGUS

As the mother of young children, I struggled. There, I said it. God had given me these remarkable creatures, perfectly formed, to love and nurture. And frankly, some days I didn't want to do it. Please don't misunderstand me. I loved my children. I simply found mothering to be the most difficult thing I had ever done—and I thought I had weathered a lot!

I left the work-for-pay world shortly after my daughter, Madison, was born. Having had my first child a little later than other mothers, I was already deeply committed to a career, and my husband and I were deeply entrenched in the lifestyle that two incomes afforded us. My job at the time of Madison's birth was a fairly intense position in a large metropolitan church. Working combined with motherhood was simply more than I wanted to do. Thinking we could easily make the necessary shifts, my husband and I decided to try the stay-at-home mom adventure.

Wow, was that a shock! Not only did we change homes to accommodate our new income level, I was thoroughly unprepared to face the nonstop world of laundry land. I was also completely uninformed about everything from the best place to get bargains to running an efficient and effective household. I had never done this before! Adding to my bewilderment, I had a perfect little baby girl whom I honestly believed was a gift from God—but I wasn't throwing myself wholeheartedly into motherhood like I had everything else I had ever done. And eventually there were two childen!

To compound my confusion and frustration, all around me seemed to be mothers who thought motherhood was the greatest thing in the world. I only had thoughts of what I would do the first day both kids were in school all day. My motto was, "I'm a great stay-at-home mom—as long as my kids are somewhere else!" I knew in my head that everything was in divine order, but emotionally and spiritually I seemed so out of whack. What was wrong with me? How did I get here? Why was I splashing around in inadequacy, guilt, and frustration?

Three Choppy Cs

Today's mother is trying to stay on board the sanity ship in the midst of three choppy Cs—choice, comparison, and competition. The crashing waves of culture and society are pounding our boats. Many of us are in an exhausting place of constantly wondering if we are doing enough for our kids, if we are doing motherhood right, if we are providing the experiences our children need, if they are dressed properly, or if we ourselves are making the grade when stacked up against all the other families, especially the mothers, in our lives.

The result? We feel intimidated, grasp for more stuff or activity, and push our kids into situations in which they are overscheduled and overwhelmed. Our children are then pressured and confused. Some are demanding and manipulative. They know we're out of control, and it breeds a sense of helplessness in them.

How did the three Cs become so storm-tossed?

Choice

The first "C" is choice. Choice itself is not necessarily bad. We base our lives around choice. It's our right, we believe, to have options. But we can also suffer from "choiceitis." With this malady, we find "each choice sprouts with its own questions. Might we? Could we? Should we? Will we? Won't we? What if we had? What if we hadn't? The forest of questions leads deeper and deeper into the dark freedom, then to the ever darker anxiety of seemingly infinite possibilities."[1] I, like many other mothers, found the array of choices baffling. On any given day, I would receive up to a dozen catalogs in the mail offering beautiful clothes, the latest in educational toys, must-have home products, and an assortment of stimulating decorations for Junior's room. Some days I could toss them all into the trash; some days I let them drag me under by wondering if I were making the best choices for my kids, my husband, and me.

We have choices in schools. We have choices in juice. We have choices in activities, daycare, breakfast cereal, fast food, denim, and churches. While it seems funny when we read the list in a book, it can be overwhelming to sort out the options and feel confident in our decisions. For instance, one of my friends described the frantic chaos of choosing the right clothing for a family portrait. She shopped in multiple stores, purchased multiple outfits for each person, had everyone try on every outfit, then returned all of the unused clothing to the stores of original purchase. She was drowning in choices.

With these infinite possibilities come the ever-present opportunities to see how our lives and choices are stacking up against others. We can drown in the continuous onslaught of society giving us options and then encouraging us to compare our decisions to the decisions other people are making.

Comparisons

The second stormy "C" is comparisons. Comparisons start right from the beginning. How were your baby's Apgar scores? Do you have Junior registered yet for the latest developmental program that will ensure he's ahead of others when he enters preschool? Did your child make the cut for the advanced placement kindergarten or the peewee all-star soccer team? And this is all before your child is five years old!

Then the church social/neighborhood party/soccer field conversation revolves around which child has made what musical/sports/academic achievement. How are Susie and Johnny's PSAT scores? How are their SAT scores? Did they get better or did they get worse? What are they going to do about getting into college? How is their litany of involvements and accomplishments measuring up against the competition?

The comparisons are not limited to what our children are doing. I would stand in grocery store lines and check out the clothing of the people around me. Hmmm, she's wearing this or that—my husband must be making more (or less) money than hers. Oh, she got her figure back so quickly after she gave birth. Not fair. Wow, her house is much prettier/bigger/cleaner than mine. Ha! My whites are whiter than hers!

I acted like one of Dr. Seuss' most famous characters, the Sneetch. As the story goes, "Half of the Sneetches have bellies with stars, and half of the Sneetches have no stars on thars." The half that doesn't have stars wants stars and the half with stars wants them off when they realize the other half is getting them. In an endless quest to have what the other half has or doesn't have, the Sneetches spend all of their money paying attention to and trying to remedy comparisons. They become obsessed with the outward appearance of things instead of focusing on the internal significance of each creature. They wind up broke and very confused. I was a Sneetch—comparison driven, confused, and going broke. No wonder I felt like I was drowning!

And the challenges of comparisons is not just a phenomenon of the secular world, where we might expect people to be focused on the apparent success a person enjoys by weighing material possessions, social status, or achievements. Comparison is alive and thriving in the Christian community as well. We compare ourselves to other mothers by how much Bible we know, how much Bible our kids know, how many times a week we're at the church, and how we are adhering to the latest standards of what a "good" Christian wife and mother looks and acts like. The religious are just as good at comparing and drawing success conclusions as the nonreligious. An insightful little story into Christ's view of religious comparisons is told in Luke 18:9-14:

> To some who were confident of their own righteousness and looked down on everybody else, Jesus told this parable: "Two men went up to the temple to pray, one a Pharisee and the other a tax collector. The Pharisee stood up and prayed about himself: 'God, I thank you that I am not like other men—robbers, evildoers, adulterers—or even like this tax collector. I fast twice a week and give a tenth of all I get.'

"But the tax collector stood at a distance. He would not even look up to heaven, but beat his breast and said, 'God, have mercy on me, a sinner.'

"I tell you that this man, rather than the other, went home justified before God. For everyone who exalts himself will be humbled, and he who humbles himself will be exalted."

The only people Jesus openly criticized in the Gospels were the religious leaders of the day who set up bogus comparisons between themselves and the rest of the community who they believed didn't live up to their expectations and rules. Perhaps the distaste Christ expressed for the religious man in the story of the Pharisee and the tax collector is a disdain for setting up false and arrogant comparisons that cause rifts between people and chasms in our ability to truly care for one another.

Money Magazine (March 19, 2002) noted the comparison epidemic. The title of the article asked, "Are You Raising a Brat?" Brats are formed as they observe what other people have and insist that they have the same thing. Today's kids are media and advertising savvy. They know how to spot knockoffs from the original brand, and they won't settle for the knockoff. Why? Because parents have taught them, or at least have not challenged the notion, that in the comparison game, only the best is noteworthy. Parents look around at what other families are providing for their children, and in an effort to protect their offspring from feeling inferior, they do whatever is necessary to ensure there will be no deficits in their education, their wardrobe, their electronics, or their opportunities. This is driven by the biggest comparison of all—we want to provide them with a "better" life than we had as children. In a recent adult education class I taught in a church, one wise mother responded, "And what was so bad about the life we had?"

Competition

In an article in the *Indianapolis Star* (March 25, 2002), entitled "Fewer Refs Still Game for the Job" by Steve Hanlon, a survey from the National Federation of High School Associations revealed that 45 percent of referees and officials for kids' athletic programs decided not to reregister because of "poor sportsmanship from coaches, spectators and/or players." The poor sportsmanship stems from people not getting what they want or feel they deserve—to win. When someone wins, someone else loses. That's the essence of competition, the third unruly "C."

Athletics have ceased to be about character building and have turned into the quest for winning titles, scholarships, and headlines. The referees, who have borne the brunt of the foul attitudes this produces, are deciding they simply won't take it anymore.

I recently heard a story about a mother who called one of her friends about cheerleading tryouts. The mother was very concerned that if their girls didn't try out for and make this particular competition squad, they wouldn't have a ghost of a chance in making the high school cheer team. The girls in question were seven years old. To make matters more intense, the mother was highly anxious because a competition squad that her first grader was already on had a cheerleading meet coming up. The cause of the anxiety? The seven-year-old wasn't able to "stick" the round off back handspring that her squad was counting on her to do to win the competition. Seven years old...

The sports field is not the only turbulent water that fosters competition. We worry if another child walks before ours does. And we gloat if our child reads before the others. If we as parents have our own unmet competition needs, we may push our uninterested children into beauty pageants or art lessons. We challenge test results that have kept our child from a particular program. While there is nothing wrong with being our child's advocate, motivation and manner can say a great deal as to whether unhealthy competition is brewing or we are simply finding the best learning style and environment for the student.

Competition is most often characterized by someone winning and someone losing. I must be right, and you must be wrong. While comparisons may be somewhat depersonalized, competition is personal. We have at stake either coming out decidedly on top or being in the wrong. Having many options or choices, coupled with our natural tendency to always be comparing ourselves to others, can naturally lead to competition. The choice I make, if threatened by someone else's opposite choice such as working outside the home for pay or staying at home and working for no pay, can lead me to feel hostile to the other "side" while adamantly protecting or defending my own choice. Sometimes, the more threatened I feel, the more adamant I become. We can drown in the choppy "C" of competition.

In *Reuters Limited* (March 15, 2003), findings of a study of 402 Australian children indicate "children who equate happiness with money, fame, and beauty are more likely to suffer from depression than youngsters who do not place as much value on being rich and attractive." Who says it only applies to children?

How Did I End Up in This Ocean?

There are two ways a mother can find herself thrown into the choppy Cs. The first and most jarring way is to be thrown overboard, to feel like you have lost touch with your special essence, your identity. Your mother ship, the S.S. Sanity, has not only tossed you over the side, the vessel itself is nowhere to be found. You are splashing around in the three choppy Cs and have no idea how you got there, who you are, and how you're going to survive.

You may feel like Gail, who was part of a planning team for a women's retreat I led. Our central passage involved Psalm 37:4: "Delight yourself in the LORD and he will give you the desires of your heart." Gail said, "That would be fine if I had any clue about the desires of my heart. The other night my two children and husband were out for the evening. I could decide what I wanted to have for dinner without any input from anyone else. When I asked myself, 'What do I really want for dinner?' I had no idea. I have no idea what I want anymore."

This type of overboard experience often begins in a transition. You have your first child, and you are now a mother. You have your second child, and you are now a mother of multiple children. You may have changed your career status as you added children. Your spouse may need to increase work hours and decrease home hours to accommodate the increased financial needs. Your relationship with your spouse has most certainly changed. Transitions, even happy transitions like birth and marriage, necessitate a change in identity. When you're drowning, you simply don't know who you are, what you want, or what you stand for anymore—and with children to care for and a household to run, there isn't much time to figure it out.

We flounder in the choppy Cs when we don't have a strong sense of our God-given identity. Without the internal strength of our own purpose, we get swept under by the purposes of others and by the norms of our culture. We need a significant rescue vessel—a good and sturdy lifeboat—to stabilize us and help us reboard the mother ship.

The second way to get thrown overboard is when we find that we simply have too much going on in life. We're frazzled. One car is on the blink, the kids have practice at two separate ends of town, the schedule is just too full, and our personal tank is just too empty. We haven't lost sight of the ship, but we're definitely in the water.

In this second type of overboard experience, we just need a few good pieces of rescue equipment and skills to help us get back on deck of the sanity ship, where we can gain perspective on how to navigate the choppy Cs instead of being tossed about by them.

Signs You May Be Going Under

Do any of these examples hit home? You may be in need of rescue!

1. *Forgetfulness.* Brenda ran her typical Monday routine with her small son. Having spent the morning running errands, she came into the house hauling her final load out of the car and proceeded with her in-house chores. Three hours later her husband came in and inquired, "Why is the car engine running?" So preoccupied with all she had to accomplish, Brenda had left the engine on after she had brought in her son and the groceries.

The constant feeling that you have to get on to the next task or that you have a hundred things to do can lead to forgetfulness in the moment. You may forget things like the PIN code at the ATM, where you put a certain object, or where you were going as you are driving down the street to appointments. This forgetfulness compounds frustration as you leave in your wake a string of half-finished tasks, then mentally condemn yourself because you just can't get anything done.

2. *Mind/body split.* Linda put it beautifully: "No matter where I am, I always think I should be at the other place." When we're volunteering at one school, we think we should be at another place or at home doing the housework. When we're at work, we think we should be volunteering in the community. When we're at home tending to house and family, we think we should be bettering ourselves by

exercising or taking an adult education course. When we're volunteering for a worthy cause, we wonder if we ought to do something for pay to help with the family finances.

3. *Inability to enjoy anything.* You are drowning if you can't enjoy simple pleasures that once brought you contentment. If you have lost the ability to see the humor in situations or you are not as engaged with your senses as you once were, you may be overwhelmed with details and comparisons, shoulds and oughts.

4. *Overwhelming need to get away.* Many were the afternoons when my husband got home from work that I wanted to brush past him to get in the car to go for a drive by myself. I didn't actually do it very often, but it was a recurring thought, especially when the children were small. I felt trapped. This sense of drowning is often expressed in the exasperated statement, "I wish I could just go to the bathroom by myself!"

5. *Feeling isolated.* Even though you have lovely friends in your life, you truly feel nobody really understands what you're experiencing. Comparisons are driving a wedge between you and others, making real connections impossible. As Laurie Cowen said, "Friendship is not possible between two women, one of whom is very well dressed." Even though you have a remarkable husband who loves to co-parent, you can't quite get him to comprehend what a day is like for you. There's nothing worse than the feeling of drowning with no one there to pull you out.

6. *Dissatisfaction with life.* If you have the feeling that nothing is quite right when it seems so right for everyone else, you may be drowning. Why can't your kids act a certain way? Why can't you find a job that will make you happy and allow you to be a terrific

wife and mother, too? Why can't you just get on with your life? Why don't you have all the things the other women in your peer group have? Or you may simply have a vague feeling that motherhood is holding you back from something more important.

7. *Inability to be quiet.* One mom said, "I have the most beautiful backyard. I would love to sit and look out the window at my flowers and the birds. But every time I sit down to look, my mind kicks into 'there are so many mothers who are doing so many things right now. What am I not doing that they are doing that would help my children get ahead, or make my house cleaner, or make my community a better place? I better get up and get to work or they'll think I'm lazy and ineffective.'"

8. *You go against your better judgment.* Your child comes home from school and says, "Why don't we have...? Why don't we go to...? How come she gets a _____ in her room and I don't?" Rather than explain your set of values, you feel you're swimming against the tide and your children are paying the price by being deprived and feeling second-rate. Since we don't want our children to think poorly of themselves, or have others look down on them, we give in and provide the missing item or experience, even though it may actually violate our own sense of propriety or necessity.

9. *You spend more than you make.* Symptom 8 often leads to Symptom 9. None of us needs to look far or deep into our society to realize that the three Cs of choice, comparison, and competition are causing havoc in family finances. Adding to the powerful undertow of accumulation is the wave-crashing force of indebtedness to keep up with what we believe everyone else has debt free. In other words, we are comparing our life to what we only *see* of another person's life.

Spending more than we make is like being the emperor who paraded around without his clothes. We have a sinking feeling that our lack is obvious, so we rush in to fill the "need." We're not willing to admit the lack, feel the discomfort, and yet take steps to be real.

10. *You feel inferior.* Comparisons always produce someone who wins and someone who loses. You may feel you are the loser. Unless, of course, you're the winner. In either case, a caring and respectful relationship with your competitor is almost impossible.

11. *You are angry.* You are angry with your children for being born. You are angry with God because he won't make your children go to sleep so you can get some, too. You are angry with your husband because he's clue free. You are angry with the woman in the next van because hers is clean. You are angry with yourself because of a hundred different lacks or excesses. You are, as Julie Ann Barnhill describes in *She's Gonna Blow,* Mount Momma, a volcano ready to erupt.*

As mothers, we are the central nervous system of our homes. As children of God, we are beautiful and necessary parts of Creation. Most importantly, as people we need and deserve to feel peaceful, poised, and confident about who we are and how we live life to the fullest. How do we go from soggy and disoriented to dry and sane?

---

* These signs you may be drowning, when they are prolonged and debilitating, can be indicators of clinical depression, an emotional disruption with a physical cause. Talk with a doctor who takes you seriously and/or a good therapist to get this treated.

Search and Rescue

1. *Warm up*—Describe a time when you felt like a mom overboard.

2. When you feel overboard, how does it affect your family? How does it feel to have that much power?

3. Think back over this past week. What choices have you made in shopping, activities, and relationships? In which choices were you confident? Which choices left you wondering if you had done the right thing?

4. In the past 48 hours, how have you compared yourself and your family members to others? How did the comparisons make you feel?

5. In what current situations are you and your family facing competition—real or imagined?

6. Which of the "Signs You May be Drowning" are most applicable to you?

7. Write a prayer to God, asking him what he wants you to know about yourself and how he feels about you. Write out his answer.

8. *Assignment for the upcoming week*—Keep the words "choice," "comparison," and "competition" where you can see them on a regular basis. When you start to feel like you're in choppy waters, ask yourself if you're sinking in one of the three Cs.

2

Navigating the Waves

The first rule is to keep an untroubled spirit. The second is to look things in the face and know them for what they are.

— MARCUS AURELIUS

There is no mistaking our situation. As women and mothers, we live in a culture and society that are going to continually produce the three choppy Cs. We are citizens of this earth, and all around us there will be choices, comparisons, and competitions constantly pounding on our ships. The good news of the gospel to which we can cling and on which we can be carried to safety, is this: We don't have to live this way! We don't have to be tossed about and sucked under as women who have no bearings and stability.

Jesus of Nazareth stated this as the center of his earthly purpose, "I have come that they may have life, and have it to the full" (John 10:10). Because I believe in Jesus' words and Jesus' purpose on my behalf, I began to search for the truth that would set me free from the powerful currents of choice, comparisons, and competition. What has God sent to rescue me when I feel like I'm overboard?

His powerful presence and authentic modeling showed the people of his day that the surest way to a puny, pitiful, painful life was to try to conform to society's demands and expectations:

> So do not worry, saying, "What shall we eat?" or "What shall we drink?" or "What shall we wear?" For the pagans run after all these things, and your heavenly Father knows that you need them. But seek first his kingdom and his righteousness, and all these things will be given to you as well (Matthew 6:31-33).

Jesus personally showed the people through his words and his works the way to live in the world but not of the world. He offers the same guidance to us today.

With love and passion, Jesus tells us stories that present new ways for people to live—ways that may contradict "religious" wisdom and the example of those for whom outward appearance is more important than inward relationship:

> Then the King will say to those on his right, "Come, you who are blessed by my Father; take your inheritance, the kingdom prepared for you since the creation of the world. For I was hungry and you gave me something to eat, I was thirsty and you gave me something to drink, I was a stranger and you invited me in, I needed clothes and you clothed me, I was sick and you looked after me, I was in prison and you came to visit me."
>
> Then the righteous will answer him, "Lord, when did we see you hungry and feed you, or thirsty and give you something to drink? When did we see you a stranger and invite you in, or needing clothes and clothe you? When did we see you sick or in prison and go to visit you?"
>
> The King will reply, "I tell you the truth, whatever you did for one of the least of these brothers of mine, you did for me" (Matthew 25:34-40).

Jesus, in his Sermon on the Mount, tells his listeners to practice compassion, charity, forgiveness, and freedom from rituals and constraints (Matthew 5–7). In other words, he urges us to see things from God's perspective instead of from the world's point of view. He encourages us to look to God for our identity and source of power.

Jesus gives his followers new eyes to see themselves as God sees them, and to view their lives as a gift from God to be lived with the constant loving presence of God. He gives us hope that what we are seeing is never all there is, and that God is graciously moving always on our behalf to draw us closer and align us more fully with his intentions for us.

By truly looking at what Jesus offers me in the words of the four Gospels (Matthew, Mark, Luke, John), I became more aware of the dynamically personal nature of Jesus' stated intention that I have life and have it abundantly. He was talking about me when he said it. He didn't say abundant life would only be available at certain points in my personal history. He didn't say abundant life was only offered if my life was picture perfect by the world's standards. He didn't say I would experience abundant life only when things were lined up just the way I think they should be. There were no qualifiers on his statement. That must mean that abundant life is available to me even at trying, stressful, and frustrating times. The rescue for the overboard outlook of my situation must be at hand.

In addition to seeking and claiming the rescue resources God provided for me, I noted the traits of women around me who were confident and peaceful in what they were doing, who were sailing and not sinking. The more I watched mothers who really seemed to enjoy what they do, the more clues I got about what it means to be a mother who has her feet firmly planted on the deck of the S.S. Sanity.

The Divine Assignment Lifeboat

The first and most striking characteristic of the confident and peaceful women I observed was they had a powerful sense of personal purpose. So taken was I by this quality that I started to research and explore where this sense of purpose comes from and how someone discovers and embraces it in her own life. I am deeply indebted to Christian writers and thinkers such as Os Guiness, John Ortberg, Richard N. Bolles, and Parker Palmer for their work in this area. I have been particularly moved by the work of Laurie Beth Jones in her book *The Path*. They helped me understand that the only way to start swimming to and reboarding the S.S. Sanity was to diligently seek and adopt what I call the *Divine Assignment*.

This major lifeboat, the Divine Assignment, is a magnificent composite of your passions, talents, interests, and circles of influence. You were designed specifically for your assignment from birth. Before you assumed any of the roles you currently play, you were born a distinct child of God and given a specific place and purpose in creation. You are significant. How does this impact your life? How can you find your Divine Assignment? In Part 2 we'll explore Divine Assignments in general and go through a step-by-step process that will enable you to begin discovering and living your own Divine Assignment.

The Essential Lifesavers

While the confidently sailing mothers have a strong sense of who they are and why they are here, I noticed they also employed certain attitudes and behaviors that helped them more easily regain their sanity if they were thrown overboard by daily distractions and ceaseless demands. These attitudes and behaviors are the dozen lifesavers highlighted here and more fully described in Part 3.

The *Beholding Lifesaver* gives you the chance to see the Divine Assignment unfolding in your children. As you realize and value the distinct contributions your children are sent to make, you can be freed from all the anxiety that comes from wondering if you're making the right choices for them, comparing them to others, and feeling like you are competing with other families in the best kid category.

The *Self-Care Lifesaver* harnesses the wise words of Jesus when he invited us to love God with all of our heart, soul, mind, and strength. Self-care is an attitude of loving God's precious creation—ourselves—enough to take care of it for maximum wholeness and effectiveness in living out our mission.

Healthy moms use the *Listening Lifesaver.* They listen to the Holy Spirit, to themselves, to their husbands, to their children, and to the wise counsel of experienced and loving people in their family and community who are truly listening to them, as well.

Confident moms swim in laughter. We need to learn how to laugh at ourselves and laugh with others. The *Laughter Lifesaver* gives us a chance to teach our children powerful lessons about God's character and grace.

Hand in hand with the Laughter Lifesaver is the *Play Lifesaver.* Play is good for us, but a very small percentage of us really feel good at it or are comfortable with it. Play helps us discover the unique child in each of us.

Moms use the *Touch Lifesaver* through kisses, hugs, and cuddles. They also know they gain and provide strength when they touch their children using the other four senses as well.

The *Recording Lifesaver* helps us enjoy the here and now, with an eye toward what will make a great memory.

A successfully sailing mother is likely to use the *Healthy Connections Lifesaver.* Moms I observed who had confidence and contentment made wise decisions about the people they chose to be with and to whom they expose their children.

Nothing will sink a mother faster than unforgiveness. The *Forgiveness Lifesaver* is fundamental for keeping our heads above water. There are many situations we find on a regular basis in which we need to forgive someone, or ourselves, for a transgression, real or imagined. There is a genuine buoyancy in the life of someone who keeps the slate free from resentment, guilt, and unexpressed anger.

Strong moms use the application of their Divine Assignment to grab the *Yes and No Lifesaver*. They make informed decisions about the many requests for their resources. They use two words commonly found in the vocabulary of their wise two-year-olds: "why" and "no."

Happy moms know their family is like no other and look for ways to use the *Celebrate Uniqueness Lifesaver*. They look for ways to nurture the distinctiveness of each family member, as well as the uniqueness of their family as a unit.

And, last, the powerful *Gratitude Lifesaver* makes a bad situation better and a good situation terrific. Moms who are good at the skill of expressing gratitude find great contentment and build a solid foundation in their homes.

Navigating the waves means first keeping our eyes and hearts centered in a loving and healthy relationship with God. When God has the principal place in our lives, we can more readily understand and use the rescue equipment and skills he has sent to ensure abundant life…which includes sanity!

Search and Rescue

1. *Warm up*—Give an example from the past week in which you felt strong and stable, beautifully sailing on the deck of the S.S. Sanity.

2. How do you respond to the news of Jesus that we don't have to drown? Relieved? Skeptical? Indifferent? Overjoyed?

3. What does it mean to you to live *in* the world but not of the world?

4. What would it mean for you, as a woman and a mother, to make God's standard the one that informs your choices, comparisons, and competitions? What do you think God's standards actually are?

5. Who have been role-model mothers for you? What qualities attracted you to them? How do you think they got them?

6. Ask God to give you a vision of peacefulness and sailing through the choppy Cs instead of floundering overboard. Write out his answer.

7. *Assignment for the upcoming week*—Notice people around you who seem to have an untroubled spirit. Ask them what their secret is.

Part 2

God Has a Unique Plan for You!

The Divine Assignment—
Your Primary Lifeboat

*The desire to fulfill the purpose for which you
were created is a gift from God.*

—A. W. TOZER

One of the most prolific and often quoted letter writers of all time wrote this advice to his good friends in ancient Galatia:

> Make a careful exploration of who you are and the work you have been given, and then sink yourself into that. Don't be impressed with yourself. Don't compare yourself to others. Each of you must take responsibility for doing the creative best you can with your own life (Galatians 6:4-5 THE MESSAGE).

The apostle Paul's wise counsel is just as powerful today as it was many years ago. What does it mean to explore who you are and discover the work you have been given? It means finding your Divine Assignment.

Understanding and living your Divine Assignment answers the questions "Why am I here?" "What does God want me to do with my life?" and "How do I creatively live my life in whatever stage I'm in?" and "How can I make the most of the role I have as a mother with children at home?" Your Divine Assignment gives you laser-focused precision to make the hundreds of decisions you make every day as a mother, a worker, a wife, a friend, a member of your extended family. Because you have many "characters" you play in a day or week's time, you need a clear filter to use as you continually seek to become more aligned with the woman God created you to be.

Common Goal, Individual Purpose

We all have common goals that are basic to being human. As mothers, we want the best for our children. As believers in God, we long for a deeper connection with him and to see his goals realized on earth as they are in heaven. If we are married, we are intentional about building and maintaining a strong and intimate relationship with our spouses. As representatives of Christ indwelt by the Holy Spirit, we know our ultimate responsibility is to love the Lord our God with all of our heart, soul, mind, and strength, and our neighbors as ourselves (Matthew 22:37-39).

God wants us to align our goals with his. While he wants us to have this intention, the individual purposes he has for each of us are as different as every individual he created. So, my friend and I may both have an intense desire to serve God, but that service will be played out quite differently in each one of us.

God's Plans Are Perfect, But What About Me?

Our Divine Assignment enables us to grasp the encouragement to "throw off everything that hinders and the sin that so easily entangles, and let us run with perseverance the race marked out for us. Let us fix our eyes on Jesus, the author and perfecter of our faith..." (Hebrews 12:1-2).

One of the greatest hindrances and entanglements we face as mothers is perfectionism. After all, Jesus mentioned this in a pesky little verse embedded in the Sermon on the Mount (Matthew 5:48): "Be perfect, therefore, as your heavenly Father is perfect." Deeply believing that God doesn't desire that I drive myself crazy trying to be something I'm not, nor ever could be, I looked into what some noted Christian thinkers had to say on this subject. William Barclay gives a healthy perspective on what "perfect" means in Greek, the language the book of Matthew is written in:

> The Greek word for perfect is *teleios*....The Greek idea of perfection is functional. A thing is perfect if it fully realized the purpose for which it was planned, and designed, and made. A thing is *teleios,* if it realizes the purpose for which it was planned; a man is perfect if he realizes the purpose for which he was created and sent to the world.
>
> Let us take a very simple analogy. Suppose in my house there is a screw loose, and I want to tighten and adjust this screw. I go out to the ironmonger and I buy a screw-driver. I find that the screw-driver exactly fits the grip of my hand; it is neither too large or too small, too rough or too smooth. I lay the screw-driver on the slot of the screw, and I find that it exactly fits. I then turn the screw and the screw is fixed. In the Greek sense, and especially in the New Testament sense, that screw-driver is *teleios,* because it exactly fulfilled the purpose for which I desired and bought it.[1]

You can be perfect as God is perfect when you discover the purpose of your birth and then live it. It will fit with who you are and what you love. That's what God is and does. He knows who he is and acts completely in accordance with his true nature. He can't do otherwise. And he created us with the same sense of who we are and our purpose.

"Perfect" also has another definition that will make it easier to embrace that we can indeed become more perfect all the time. In the Old Testament book of Deuteronomy, Moses writes this strange little verse: "You must be blameless before the LORD your God" (18:13). I find that to be quite a tall order. Does that mean I can't commune with God until I'm without fault or imperfection? John Calvin cleared this up for me when he explained that "perfect" simply means I keep my eyes focused on God and don't get caught up in worldly things that can draw my attention away from serving God with the joy that comes from knowing my Divine Assignment, that is, knowing who I am and whose I am.

In addition to being a perfect fit, a Divine Assignment is...

○ *A partnership.* One reason I so often found myself drowning was I was trying to live my life and find my identity in myself, my outward material possessions, and relationships. Even though I was raised a "Christian," I was relatively clue free regarding the graciousness of God in calling me to be and do something that was completely in alignment with what he created me to be and do. Further, I had no idea of the wonderful relationship I could enjoy with the Holy Spirit of Christ on a moment-by-moment basis. Mostly I had grown to believe that God was scary, aloof, and wanted me to take all of my natural gifts, interests, skills, and passions and get rid of them. That meant I was "bearing my cross and denying myself." But the truth is that God gave me all of those things and simply asked that I align them with his power and intention for the two of us to bring something magnificent to his world.

◯ *A healing for you.* Time and again as I have coached individuals and groups through the process of discovering their Divine Assignment, I have seen God's mercy to individuals first. For example, in a group I led for a church close to my home, we met for five weeks to give the women a chance to thoroughly process and discuss what they were learning. One woman realized that her Divine Assignment was "God's Acceptance," and she believed she was to spread that good news to others in her life. She struggled over our weeks together with what that meant for her to do in her life. Then one evening I said, "Your Divine Assignment applies first to you, and then to the others in your life." The impact of that statement brought her to tears as she realized she needed to fully embrace God's acceptance of her first, before she tried to spread it to the world. The truth came home to rest as she realized that was the only way she was going to be able to genuinely live her Divine Assignment.

◯ *A healing for others.* Your call will authentically benefit others, as well. We have all been created in the image of God. God's ultimate image is restoration, benevolence, light, and life. Your ultimate call is to the same. How this call is lived out in each person is as individual as the people themselves. But people will be healed by your presence, by the essence of who you are as you are genuinely living your purpose, not by all the things you think you "should" be doing to benefit the world.

◯ *A stretching.* John Ortberg wrote a compelling book called *If You Want to Walk on Water, You've Got to Get Out of the Boat.* In it he explores getting out of our spiritual comfort zone to where we begin to feel nervous or uncomfortable. This is completely purposeful on God's part. If we weren't nervous or uncomfortable, we would rely on ourselves to accomplish our Assignment. Ortberg's wise advice is, "Never try to have more faith—just get to know God better. And because God is faithful, the better you know him, the more you'll trust him."[2]

○ *A dynamic call.* God is never boring or static. His Assignment for you will most certainly be tweaked from time to time. You will sense your call shifting over a long period of time as you and your family change. That's because God wants you to remember to walk intimately with and dependently on him every step of the way. He wants you to keep checking in and watching his hand.

There are some things your Divine Assignment is *not…*

○ *One size fits all.* Early in my marriage, driving around the Beltway in the metropolitan Washington, D.C., area with my new husband, I whined, "But what makes me special?" He answered, "You're special because you are a child of God." "That's not special," I retorted. "Everyone is a child of God." As we struggled along with this conversation for a few more rounds, we discovered that what I wanted to know was what made me, Robin Chaddock, distinct. What was my unique contribution to the world? We all want to know how we make an impact. And we all have a distinct place in this world. As one of my friends put it, "If we were both alike, one of us would be dispensable." Your Divine Assignment is unique to you.

○ *A luxury.* It's tempting to think that a Divine Assignment is only for those who can afford to "not work." We may think,

I have to put food on the table and keep this household running. I don't have time for meaning. We're trying to survive here. Your Divine Assignment is *how* you do what you do as much as it is something you do. It's not exclusively for the leisure class. Your Divine Assignment is given to you based especially on where you are at this place in time and at this spot on the planet.

◑ *A deep, dark secret.* A story is told of a bunch of Greek gods sitting around bemoaning the fact that if humans discover their own destinies, they'll become like the gods. The gods like having a monopoly on that identity, so they begin to plot where they'll hide these destinies so the humans can't find them. One says, "I know. Let's put them in the sky. They'll never find them there." "No," say the rest of the gods, "they love their sunsets and constellations and cloud formations. They'll find their destinies there too soon." So another god says, "I know. Let's put their destinies in the ocean. They'll be safe there." But the other gods say, "No, they love swimming and seafood and communing with water. They'll find them quickly there, as well." So the gods sit around pulling on their beards and scratching their heads. Then one gets a powerful gleam in his eye and says, "I know. Let's hide their destinies inside of them, in their hearts. They'll never think to look there!" And sure enough, many of us don't. We don't think to look there because we're waiting for someone to give us permission to trust ourselves and God's working in our lives. But our Divine Assignment can be as close as our heartbeat if we look and listen.

◑ *Dependent on your circumstances.* You are never in a place where you cannot live your Divine Assignment. It's not a job or a relationship or a role that you have to find or capture. You can live it even if you're paralyzed on a bed in the middle of nowhere with few people around.

○ *Grandiose or earth-shattering.* Your Assignment doesn't have to change the entire world. In fact, that is one of the biggest misunderstandings about call and passion. We have all seen evidence of others we read about or see in the media who have accomplished very noteworthy and public purposes. We can be deceived to think we don't have a purpose because we aren't as famous and remarkable as they are. The truth is, if we don't play our note, there's a hole in the symphony of life. Those feelings of insignificance only betray our tendency to compare and compete with others.

Robust Rescue Craft

The Lifeboat of a well-defined Divine Assignment helps us swim through the three choppy Cs (choice, comparisons, competition) and safely reboard the S.S. Sanity. It puts all of our choices into perspective. Once we know why we are here, we can effectively and serenely say yes and no to all of the options and opportunities that come to us and to members of our family. As one of my coaching clients said, "When I have been making choices about how we spend our time and energy, even money, I ask myself if it fits into my purpose. Are we doing activities or buying things that serve a purpose or just blowing time and money without thought?" Another mom who discerned her Divine Assignment says her life has become more centered and calm. She knows when to accept or decline an invitation to serve at school, in the community, or through the church. She has cut away the involvements that don't help her accomplish her Assignment, while being open to and focused on the many chances she has to actively live her purpose.

Embracing our Divine Assignment helps us effectively meet the comparison challenge simply because we realize there is no one created with our distinct purpose. Many comparisons have an outward, materialistic base. The power of our Divine Assignment is that it takes us to a deeper, more authentic playing field where we understand we each have our own part to play. The big picture is incomplete without our unique input. Each person is here for a reason, and the greatest joy is to get on with our God-given Divine Assignment and forget about energy-wasting comparisons.

Standing at the check-in for a beautiful hotel in which I was staying as the speaker for a church-based retreat, I noticed a flyer on the desk for an upcoming retreat the hotel was sponsoring. The picture of the speaker was lovely, so I picked up the brochure to check out her credentials. *Sigh.* She had written six more books than I had and had been on the cover of a well-known Christian magazine for women. I had to fight that instinctive and instantaneous urge to feel like a loser in comparison. Thankfully, I could pull myself together as the Holy Spirit reminded me of my Divine Assignment and the truth that God has all of us where he wants us, when he wants us there. End of internal discussion!

Discerning and living our Divine Assignment gives us the perspective we need to deal effectively with debilitating competition. The heart of unhealthy competition is the fear that losing means we won't have something we need or want. Many unhealthy competitions set us against other people. Drawing closer to our Assignment aligns us more closely with God. We understand God's grace, providence, and ability to care for us. In utilizing this Lifeboat we realize that since we are uniquely created to make a difference, others must be created likewise. Human beings become allies and partners to be respected and congratulated, not adversaries to be feared and conquered. God is sufficient for all of us. We are each and all significant.

No Call Without a Caller

The bottom line that makes the Divine Assignment Lifeboat so potent is that we can never be called without a Caller. As noted by Os Guinness, "We are not primarily called to do something or go somewhere; we are called to *Someone*. We are not first called to special work but to God. The key to answering the call is to be devoted to no one and to nothing above God himself."[3] As God said to the nation of Israel, "I have summoned you by name" (Isaiah 43:1). God has also called you first to be in a deeply loving relationship with him. Then you can more easily see the heart of God's intention for your purpose on earth. Called to God first; called to God's purpose second. The only way to put choice, comparisons, and competition in perspective is to play to the audience of One.

A mother of three children beautifully articulated the power of understanding her purpose in relationship to her walk with God:

> Since I have identified God's purpose for me, our family life is much more peaceful. I now recognize when my heart is pure versus when it is not. I more readily relinquish control and surrender to God's will, trusting him to handle all those curve balls that come my way. I guess that by finding God's purpose for my life, I have gotten to know God and myself on a deeper level. Before I identified my purpose, I lived life based on *my* experiences. I always felt like something was missing. I would go out and live my life independently and come back and show God what I did or did not do. What I have learned

was missing was a moment-by-moment partnership with God. Now I try to never leave his presence.

Your Divine Assignment is made of four parts: Central Passion, Strength, Interests, and Circles of Influence. In the next two chapters we will discover what each of these means for you. You *can* know who you are, why you're here, and what you want to do with that information!

Search and Rescue

1. *Warm up*—What one word most describes you at this very point in time?

2. Are you a perfectionist? What new understanding did you find in the word "perfect" in this chapter?

3. As you prepare to discover your Divine Assignment, there are a few clarification strategies for you to go through first.

    a. Respond to this quote: "One of the worst reasons to follow a particular path in life is that other people want you to."

    b. As you ponder the quote, write your personal definition of success, and include the areas of finance, health, relationships, spirituality, vocation, and recreation.

    c. Write a piece of Hebrew-styled poetry about yourself. In Proverbs 31, the woman described is written in the form of a Hebrew poem in which they used the letters of their alphabet as starting points for all of her characteristics. Write down the side of a piece of paper our English alphabet, and for each letter write a positive character trait, passion, gift, or interest you have.

4. Consider and respond to this thought: "You are the mother that God assigned to your children. Your unique Divine Assignment is part of the reason they were given to you. If you don't know or don't apply your Assignment to your mothering, you are robbing your children of something significant God has in their divine curriculum."

5. Ask God why he gave you the passions and interests he has given you. Write out his answer.

6. *Assignment for the upcoming week*—Make a note of the times in the week when you feel happy and satisfied. What are you doing at those points?

Discovering Your Divine Assignment

Learn what you are and be such.

—PINDAR

Claudia was a very active volunteer in her community. She had remarkable organizational skills, plenty of creative vision, and excellent communication savvy that made her a sought-after chairperson and event planner. Yet she was getting tired, and she sometimes found herself in situations she wished she had said no to. Between being involved at her church, attending school functions for her three kids, and participating in many neighborhood activities, she was spread too thin and not giving as much attention to what she felt deep down was really important—her faith, her health, and her family. Claudia needed clarity on her Divine Assignment.

Paul's Words Make Sense for Moms

In the next two chapters, we will flesh out Paul's terrific counsel to his Galatian friends. It turns out to be a sure and sturdy Lifeboat to moms overboard, as well. In this chapter we will focus on making a careful exploration of who you are and the work you've been given to do. Chapter 5 gives you great tools for incorporating that knowledge and understanding into your life.

As we explore Divine Assignments, please realize that this is a *process* and *takes a little time*. Don't be frustrated with yourself if you need to ponder the exercises a little bit. At the same time, don't get bogged down making it perfect. Write in pencil so you have freedom to erase. Discovering your Divine Assignment is a process you are entering into with the Holy Spirit. You can take some time trying on words and talking them over with God as you get more clarity.

Who Are You and What Have You Done with My Sanity?

One of the most common complaints when a mom falls overboard is, "I just don't feel like myself anymore. I used to be so confident, organized, energetic, happy. I just don't know who I am or what I'm about these days." There is a kernel of identity in each of us—a nugget of enthusiasm that makes us who we are. This is called our *Central Passion*.

Central Passion is not something we do. Central Passion is who we are. We start here. Many times we are so focused on doing that we forget to be. All of our best doing will stem from our best being. Knowing who we are makes us more energized to do what we do. Let's get specific.

Words for your Central Passion are those that describe qualities or core values. They are found in scripture passages such as the fruit of the Spirit: love, joy, peace, patience, kindness, goodness, gentleness, and faithfulness. They are words that echo character traits of God: justice, humor, mercy, forgiveness, wisdom. They are words that reflect the hallmarks of Christian character: hope, faith, joy, compassion, hospitality, grace.

Central Passion words are also found in common-sense traits, such as the ones found in the character code of my daughter's school: honesty, perseverance, courage, caring, initiative, responsibility, loyalty. Central Passions can be described with words we find in popular literature of growth: simplicity, safety, creativity, wholeness, and wellness.

So how do we tap this Central Passion?

Your Central Passion can be discovered by addressing two ideas found in Frederick Buechner's definition of call: "The kind of work God usually calls you to is the kind of work (a) that you need most to do and (b) that the world most needs to have done. The place God calls you to is the place where your deep gladness and the world's deep hunger meet."[1] So ask yourself, "What is my deep gladness, my Central Passion?" Give it a name from the lists in the previous paragraphs. Or let your intuition bring one to mind that most describes you. Then look at your world and ask what it is people around you most need. What is lacking that would make the world a better place for everyone? Somewhere in the overlapped answers of these two questions you can find the kernel that is your Central Passion.

This process may take some time. You may need to choose several Central Passions to try on for a few days. You might want to look up words in a dictionary or thesaurus to get a better understanding of what they mean.

As Theresa went through this process she discerned her Central Passion to be Goodness. She made this discovery in a group setting surrounded by women who had known her for a while. When the others in the group heard her say her Central Passion out loud, they all spontaneously burst out with, "That's it! That is so you!" That's one way you know you have hit the nail on the head—when others who know you respond so enthusiastically to the word you have chosen.

Another clue that you are hitting the mark is if you find yourself tearing up or your voice gets choked when you are telling others
what the word means to you. Many of the women with whom I
have gone through this process find themselves unexpectedly but
genuinely crying as the power of their unnamed essence comes to
the surface. It feels so good to be able to say, "This is who I am."

Put It to Work

After you discover and reclaim your Central Passion, you want
to find the "work you've been given." You want to apply your Passion to yourself and your world. There are three ways to discover the
work you've been given. We will tap your Strength, Interests, and
Circles of Influence.

Your Strength can also be thought of as a gift. It is an activity or
attitude that you have engaged in your whole life. If you look back
over your life, you can say, "I've always done this, no matter where
I have been." You find you did it in the sandbox, and when you
went to middle school and high school. You have probably done it
in any job you've had, whether it was part of the job description or
not. No matter where you've been, with whom you have been, or
what you've been doing, you've been doing this.

This is how you choose your Strength. Write down a list of
words that describe what you do in life. Do you motivate, ignite,
stimulate, empower, or enlist? Maybe you're more behind the scenes
and encourage, develop, advocate, support, nurture, or facilitate.
Maybe you're the kind that really gets things going and you ignite,
envision, initiate, or organize. Maybe you have a more playful spirit
and you celebrate, enjoy, praise, or plant. Is your Strength found in
communication words like write, speak, teach, verbalize, illuminate,
or describe? Maybe you're the role-model type and you exemplify,
embody, inspire, influence, or radiate. Narrow your list down to five

words, spend some time mulling over these words, looking them up if you like, and trying them on for fit. Then choose the one that resonates the most with you.

Now, enormous power can be unleashed when Passion meets Strength. When you pair your Central Passion word with your Strength word, you get a two-word phrase that can make your heart beat faster and can cause you to say with power, "That's it! That's what I was born to do!" As I have worked through this process myself, trying on lots of word combinations, I have discerned that my Divine Assignment is to Stimulate Wholeness. My Central Passion is Wholeness; my Strength is Stimulate. Together they give my life clarity, power, and meaning. I've boarded the Lifeboat and headed back to the S.S. Sanity!

The work you've been given to do also includes your Interests. Interests is the part of the Divine Assignment that gives you big clues as to what God may be wanting you to do at this particular point in time with the Central Passion and Strength he has given you. Identifying your Interests is what makes you very unique in your call. Interests can be defined as hobbies, skills, talents, and causes that you believe in.

On a separate sheet of paper, write the letters of the alphabet down one side. Use these letter prompts to brainstorm skills, talents, and causes that excite you. This is a place to list things that people say, "Oh, you're so good at…" but only if it's something you like doing, as well. For instance, I had people tell me for years I was talented at administration and organization. But I hate doing those things, so I wouldn't include them on my list. This is all about you and your preferences, joys, and loves. Please include things you don't necessarily feel you have time for right now but that still fit this definition of Interests.

Finally, the work you've been given to do includes people. Recall that in the last chapter, we identified that a Divine Assignment will be beneficial to you and to others. The next piece of your Divine Assignment puzzle identifies the people you will most impact as you are living the life you've been called to live. This is best done as a set of concentric Circles of Influence, starting with yourself in the middle.

Concentric circles look like a target for archery practice. On a separate sheet of paper, draw an archery target with three or four circles and label the central circle "Me." From there you will identify all kinds of people in your life—some very close to your core, and others who you influence on a periodic, less frequent basis. A typical set of concentric circles for a mom will include herself first at the very center, then her family, then perhaps coworkers or neighbors, then the church community or school community.

With this set of circles, you ask yourself, "As I apply my Divine Assignment to my life, who are the people God has given me to impact at this point in time?" Run through each of your circles, applying the core of the Assignment—your Central Passion and your Strength. For example, I look at each Circle of Influence I have and ask myself, "How do I Stimulate Wholeness in myself, my family, my clients, and my readers?" We all have lots of roles and relationships, and the key to effectively boarding the Divine Assignment Lifeboat is to see each role and relationship in light of who we now know ourselves to be and the work we have been given to do.

As Patti went through the process, she realized her Divine Assignment is to Encourage Flourishing. At first she was really excited by this as she envisioned all the young mothers she wanted to share her call and passions with. She spent several months trying to put together a group at her church that would help her do this. The group met a few times, but it became apparent that it was not the right time for this endeavor. Patti was deeply disappointed, and her spirit was troubled for a few months as she tried to discern what God wanted for her in this Divine Assignment.

One autumn morning after her kids were off to school, Patti was spending some quiet moments with God. "God, what in the world do you want me to do with this Divine Assignment if the women at church aren't going to make use of the group?" she questioned. Then something on her bulletin board caught her eye. It was a list of some qualities of a contented mother. Patti realized in reading the list that she wasn't tending to her own flourishing. She was so busy wanting to encourage flourishing in others, trying to "save the world" as she put it, that she hadn't looked at the center of her concentric circle to find the person God most wanted to affect with her Divine Assignment—herself.

Later that week, as she was relating this story to me, we both got a laugh out of the notion that God loves us first. Sometimes we are so caught in the mind-set that we are supposed to always put ourselves last that we forget that God always puts us first. God doesn't mind if we do the same. Being the first beneficiary of your Divine Assignment is sheer genius on the part of the Almighty. Only then can you realistically and authentically spread your Divine Assignment to your family and to those in the other circles you influence.

Three Remarkable Women

Claudia, the mom who opened this chapter, discovered the core of her Divine Assignment was Ignite Compassion. Once she realized the power this gave her to identify who she really was and the work she had been given to do, she could cut away all the commitments and responsibilities that didn't fit with her Divine Assignment. She identified her major interests and asked herself what it meant for her to Ignite Compassion in herself, her family, and others around her. Claudia became much more focused and much less stressed.

Theresa, who identified her Divine Assignment as Encourage Goodness, realized she needed to start being good to herself first. She is a very involved wife and mother of three, with one child who has special needs and considerations. She recognized that she needed to encourage a bunch of goodness in her own life in the form of self-care. Then she went on to the next circle, which is her family. She is particularly interested in her children knowing and showing goodness in their own lives. Then, as she began to catch a wider vision of her Divine Assignment, she became aware that God is calling her to other kids in the community who need to know and show goodness. Her vision is still unfolding, but it begins with goodness being central to her life and a top priority for how she mothers her children.

Likewise, Libby discovered her Central Passion is Dignity and her Strength is Safeguard. Her Divine Assignment is to Safeguard Dignity. When I asked her how this affects her mothering, she said, "When I go to discipline the kids or even start to lose my temper, it pops into my head that I want to protect their dignity." Libby's job and volunteer activities also stem from her Divine Assignment to Safeguard Dignity. She discovered her call extended to bringing dignity to foster children, especially as they prepare to enter adulthood and be released from the foster care system. The past two years she has spent researching and developing a not-for-profit business that will help her live out her Divine Assignment. Had she not gotten clear on who she is and the work she has been given to do, she would not have found this mission that helps her feel fully alive and complete.

You are a remarkable woman, too. You are a remarkable woman who just needs the words and clarity to express what you know deep down inside. God is excited for you to discover this Lifeboat of Divine Assignment, because he knows it will bring you closer to him as you celebrate your unique life.

Search and Rescue

The Search and Rescue is a bit different for this time. Fill in the blanks with the information you gained as you went through this chapter.

My Central Passion is _____, and my Strength is _____. When I combine them, I find that I am called to_____(Strength)_____ ____(Central Passion)____.

In living this Divine Assignment, I want to use my Interests in _____, _____, _____, and _____. This Divine Assignment is first applied to me, then meant to impact my Circles of Influence, which are _____, _____, _____, and _____.

For example, my Divine Assignment reads: My Central Passion is Wholeness, and my Strength is Stimulate. When I combine them I find I am called to Stimulate Wholeness. In living this Divine Assignment, I want to use my Interests in communicating, walking, consulting, and rubber-stamping. This Divine Assignment is first applied to me, then meant to impact my Circles of Influence, which are my husband, my children, my clients, and my extended family and friends.

Assignment for this week—Make multiple copies of your Divine Assignment. Keep one in your purse, your briefcase, your diaper bag, and by the phone. Tape one to the computer monitor, the dashboard, and the bathroom mirror. Look at it as many times as you can, letting it sink into your heart and mind. Become saturated with what you have just learned and let the Holy Spirit confirm it and enliven it in you. Congratulations! Discovering your Divine Assignment, Central Passion, and Strength is hard work!

5

A View from the Bow

Remember always that you have not only the right to become an individual, you have an obligation to be one. You cannot make any useful contribution in life unless you do this.

—ELEANOR ROOSEVELT

O nce the Divine Assignment Lifeboat has returned you to the S.S. Sanity, it's time to climb back up on deck and see where you are going. Imagine yourself at the captain's wheel with the breeze blowing your hair and the salt air tingling your nose. You look out over the ocean and realize you need to chart your course and consider the possibilities. You are receiving and creating a vision.

As you receive and create your vision, you are completing the apostle Paul's prescribed process in Galatians—you are discerning how to strengthen and encourage who you are and the work you've been given to do.

The Vision-Message

Habakkuk 2:2-3 (THE MESSAGE) says:

> And then GOD answered: "Write this,
> Write what you see.

Write it out in big block letters
    so that it can be read on the run.
This vision-message is a witness
    pointing to what's coming.
It aches for the coming—it can hardly wait!
    And it doesn't lie.
If it seems slow in coming, wait.
    It's on its way. It will come right on time."

Your Divine Assignment will impact you and all those around you. So ask yourself, "What will this world look like as I pass through it living my Divine Assignment?" This is the process of writing the "vision-message" in big block letters so you will have it always before you to help you make decisions about your life as seen through the lenses of your true identity.

Three Time Frames for Vision

This "vision-message," as Habakkuk calls it, can be thought of as your future self calling to your current self with the roadmap for accomplishing what you have been sent here to accomplish. One woman who went through the process with me described it as her future autobiography. Other translations of Habakkuk call the vision a "revelation." Our vision is revealed in stages, some short range, some medium range, and some long range. We can be working from all three at any one time.

Figuring out your vision-message isn't as intimidating as it might sound. I'll take you through the three stages so that you will be able to write your own vision at the end of this chapter.

Envisioning the short range gives you the opportunity to ask, "In the next three to six months, what would I like to see stay the same? What's working for me that is bringing me abundant life?

What would I like to see change? What's not working for me and is not bringing me abundant life?" In this time frame, you look at health issues you may need to address, relationships that need attention, and things you want to learn to help you carry out your Divine Assignment more effectively. For example, as I led a retreat using the process, one of the mothers realized that part of her long-range vision included establishing a Christian school in her community. Her short-range vision included researching how other people had done this in their own communities, looking at the governmental guidelines for setting up a school, and beginning to identify her resources for carrying out the vision.

In the medium-range plan, you look a little further out. What transitions do you foresee in the next six months to three years? For example, one mother I worked with on her Divine Assignment came to me specifically because she was planning ahead for the next couple years when her children would all be in school full-time. She was asking herself the question "What's next?" and wanted to get a clearer picture of what God was calling her to as she prepared to enter this new phase of her life. In the "Search and Rescue" section, there are questions for you to ponder and answer as you think about this six-month to three-year time frame.

Finally, in the long-range portion of visioning, you have the opportunity to ask and answer the question "For what do I want to be remembered?" As you envision your eightieth birthday roast, what do you want people to be saying about you, your contributions, your character, your life?

As you are writing your vision, please heed the following guidelines:

○ *Let the words flow.* Don't censor whether your vision is "possible" or worry about how it is going to be accomplished. As you write with the help of the Holy Spirit, it is your job to articulate "what" and let God take care of the "how."

◑ *Be very descriptive in your writing.* Use all of your senses. What do your surroundings look like? What do you smell and hear? Who are you talking to and about what? What tastes are you experiencing? This is called "vivid visioning." The more you can be specific, the more your mind and heart know where they are headed.

◑ *Write your visions as journal entries.* Write your vision-message in the present tense as if what you are describing has already happened or is happening as you write. Set a date on the page and write about that particular day.

One of my coaching clients wrote this vision during the work we did together as she discovered her Divine Assignment. I asked if I could share it because it is a sterling example of vision writing. (And this was from a woman who initially protested, "I can't even write a proper sentence.")

I get up on a beautiful, sunny summer day. The kids aren't up yet. I get a cup of coffee and head out onto the back deck to enjoy some quiet time to myself. It's warm and the birds are singing. Because it's early morning and quiet in the neighborhood, I can hear the hum of the traffic on I-69. I enjoy seeing the leaves on the trees and smelling the new-mown grass. The birds are really enjoying the birdfeeder. Everything sparkles in the sun—the grass, the flowers, the water in the kiddie pool. It's a jewel-like day. I thank God for the beautiful day and the beauty and peace surrounding me.

My son comes out to join me on the deck, and then we go back inside for breakfast. My daughter comes downstairs, too, and we eat our Froot Loops and toast and talk about what we want to do that day. We decide to go to the park to play. On the way there, we stop at Wendy's and get lunch to take to a picnic table in the park. When we get there we have our picnic, and the kids play on the equipment. I sit at a table and read a little bit while they play. After a while, we go over to the carousel and ride it. We get some popcorn in their little concession stand and feed some to birds when we're finished with it. Then we wander down some of the paths in the park and end up near the train museum. We look at the train cars through the fence and talk about what it's like to ride a train.

When we're done at the park, we start for home. We run a few errands and also stop at the custard stand for some ice cream. We sit in the sun at their tables and enjoy the gorgeous day. We talk and enjoy our ice cream together. After we get home, the kids go play outside, and I get some things done inside, including starting dinner.

My husband comes home a little early because I have to get to ABATE (a motorcycle safety course) by 4:30. I eat something before I leave and say goodbye to everyone. I put on my leather jacket and gloves, get on my bike (a Harley Fat Boy), and ride over there. I love the feel of the rumble and the powerful sound the engine makes. Everyone turns to see it and is surprised when it's a woman on it. I smile back at them and pull away. When I get to ABATE, I park over with the other instructors' bikes. I help get all the bikes out of the trailer and set them up in rows. We check to make sure they all run and set up the classroom. I have to present my portion of the class tonight, so I make sure I have all my information together and the video is working.

The class begins, and we get everyone on the bikes right away. Tonight we work on doing the figure eights that always scare everyone. But they are surprised to find that it's not hard, and it's fun, too. It gives them confidence in their timing. After we've worked outside for a while, we head inside the trailer for a classroom session. It's evening and the heat is starting to go down a bit, but we still have the air conditioning running in the trailer. Everyone gets a drink from the machine and settles down for class. My portion goes well, and I'm able to answer everyone's questions.

As the class comes to a close, the sun is finally going down. It's almost 9 P.M. and the sky is streaked with red. We can hear the crickets in the field next to us and the warm grass smells good as the ground mist rises. The other instructors and I take the class tables down and run the bikes up inside the trailer. We've done this a lot so we can finish quickly. By 9:20, everything is locked up. Some students had hung around and talked to some of us, and the last few cars are pulling out of the lot. We each get on our bikes and pull off into the night.

On the way home, I enjoy the smells of the ride. I've always enjoyed that. The heat is coming off the engine and feels good around me in the coolness of the evening. I stop at a stoplight and again enjoy the stares of people who didn't expect a woman on that bike. I downshift into first gear while waiting for the light to turn green and the sound of that click makes me happy deep down inside. I finish the ride home and back the bike into its spot in the garage. I go inside.

The kids are in bed and my husband is waiting for me. We sit on the back deck and end the day the way it began—

enjoying the peace and nature in the backyard. We watch Bruce (the bat that likes to hunt under the trees in our backyard), drink iced tea, and talk about our day. It's been a really, really soul-good day.

Carolyn's Central Passion is Happiness, and her vision outlines the ways her Divine Assignment touches her life, the lives of her family members, and the lives of her colleagues and students. Her vision encompasses several times of the day, highlights her Circles of Influence, is rich in sensory imagery, and is written in the present tense. You should have seen her face as she read it to me in my office.

My own story regarding vision writing is nothing short of amazing to me. When I first began to write the vision and trust God's revelations to me, I wrote at one point, "The publisher called today and wanted to know what project I'm working on next." At that point I didn't have a publisher, had only spoken with one publisher at a writer's conference, and didn't have the foggiest notion what the next project was. But I saw the vision, and I wrote it down.

Four years after writing that in my vision journal, I went to Fort Wayne, Indiana, for a radio interview and book signing of my second book, *Come to Your Senses*. The radio interviewer had three authors to interview that day, and the first one ran over by about seven minutes. I was feeling a little cheated, but decided to just be grateful that I had gotten an interview in the first place. The interviewer was a wonderful woman and she gave me seven extra minutes on my interview. All three authors were being interviewed by phone, so the last author to be interviewed heard the last seven minutes of my interview as he patiently waited his turn. At the end of my interview, the interviewer graciously allowed me to give my website address, and then I was off to my book signing.

After I finished in Fort Wayne, I drove home. As is my custom when I walk in the door, I went right to the email. I love email. As I scanned the new postings, I noticed one I didn't recognize, but it looked interesting from the subject line.

I opened the email to discover it was from a man named Terry Glaspey, an acquisitions editor for Harvest House Publishers. He had been the third author to be interviewed and had heard the last seven minutes of my interview—seven minutes that he wouldn't have heard if all had been on schedule! He indicated that he had heard me on the radio, liked the way I expressed myself, and wondered if I had a project in the works on which perhaps we could join forces. It "just so happened" that I was working on the proposal for this book. In several months' time, we realized Harvest House Publishers and *Mom Overboard* were a good match.

My vision four years earlier had set the stage for me to be ready when the time came. I had seen the "what," and it was up to God to produce the "how." While I still nearly fell out of my chair when I opened the email, and just about jumped out of my skin when I got the call that Harvest House wanted to publish this book, I was, deep inside, not surprised at all because God had shown me the vision and had me write it down several years beforehand.

I hope you can feel a bit of energy just reading about this process and glimpsing the outcome. Vision brings us vitality and the realization that what we see is never all there is. Charles Swindoll gives a stirring recommendation for allowing vision to be central to your life:

> Vision—it is essential for survival. It is spawned by faith, sustained by hope, sparked by imagination, and strengthened by enthusiasm. It is greater than sight, deeper than a dream, broader than an idea. Vision encompasses vast vistas outside

the realm of the predictable, the safe, the expected. No wonder we perish without it.[1]

We flounder in the open water without vision, too. So get up on the deck of your ship, chart a course, and sail strongly through the choppy Cs.

Search and Rescue

1. *Warm-up*—What does Charles Swindoll's quote at the end of the chapter mean to you?

2. Write your short-range vision. Refer back to pages 61-62 for the recommendations on vision writing. As you are writing your short-range vision, answer these questions: In the next month to six months, what would I like to see stay the same? What would I like to see change? How will my Divine Assignment guide me? Are there blocks that need to be removed, health issues that need to be addressed, relationships that need to be dealt with?

   In this section it is time to ask yourself, What is healthy about my life right now and what is unhealthy? What is working and what is obsolete? What is bringing me a deep sense of peace and what is bringing me disharmony?

3. In the middle-range vision, you are painting a picture of how your life and the lives of those around you will be affected as you are living your Divine Assignment. What transitions do you foresee in the next six months?

Take a look at and answer the following questions: What skills, interests, and passions do I want to be using on a regular basis? What will be my principle "product" or contribution (e.g., art, business, strong relationships, influence, community involvement)? What kind of person do I want to be (e.g., powerful, helpful, solitary, influential, "stage hand")? In what type of community do I want to live? With whom do I want to live? Give a detailed description of a typical day, both weekday and weekend, from the time you get up to the time you go to bed.

4. In the long-range vision, you have the opportunity to ask and answer the question "For what do I want to be remembered?" Address the following topics: family, community, friends, relationship with God, finances, career or life work, health, attitudes, and outlook.

5. Respond to this quote by Abraham Lincoln: "The best thing about the future is that it only comes one day at a time."

6. Write a prayer of personal dedication to God. Acknowledge places where you feel hesitant to become aligned with his Divine Assignment for you. Write out his answer.

7. *Assignment for the upcoming week*—Relax and breathe. You have all the tools you need to reboard the S.S. Sanity with your identity intact. Realize this is a process and will take time, but you now have this rescue equipment well in hand.

Part 3

Lifesavers–
Actions and Attitudes to Keep You Afloat

6

The Beholding Lifesaver

Every child is born a genius.

—ALBERT EINSTEIN

Did you see the commercial that depicts a mother, a father, and a baby preparing to go out to run errands on a Saturday morning? Actually, the mother and father were preparing to go out, the baby was sitting in the high chair watching them run in and out of the door carrying all of the items they would need for a morning away from the house. Bottles? Check. Diaper bag? Check. Educational toys for the backseat? Check. Stroller? Check. After several more trips with all of the accessories babies seem to need for an outing, the parents ran out the door, turned the key in the lock, and started the car in the driveway. Moments later they reentered the kitchen each with a look on their face that acknowledged they were goof balls. As they unstrapped and lifted the wide-eyed child, they said, "Baby. Check."

It's not so far-fetched really, to be so busy running around doing all the things that come with having children that we forget the children. Not that we actually leave them at home when we think we're driving them to practice or lessons, but we just forget there are actual human beings in the growing bodies we are providing for and carting everywhere.

Children as Beans

The wonderful wisdom handbook, the book of Proverbs, has this advice for parents, "Train a child in the way he should go, and when he is old he will not turn from it" (22:6). While that has historically been understood to mean the way of "spare the rod, spoil the child" punishment, I believe there is another, more nurturing and life-changing interpretation.

My father loves to plant a garden each year. He sows tomatoes, pumpkins, and zucchini. He plants lots of marigolds around the perimeter to keep away the little pests. The one crop that is the most challenging to manage is green beans. They grow everywhere and would take over the whole patch if not for one wise gardening move. My father stakes them to keep them from becoming a nuisance. He helps them be the best they can be so we're glad they're in the garden, and so we can enjoy their unique essence when the time comes to eat fresh beans all summer.

As a stake helps the green beans, or a ditch helps the flow of water, encouraging the dynamic unfolding of children's natures requires we know who they are and bring them the experiences and support they need to be the best they can be. We need to recognize children have a purpose, a specific reason for having been born.

To be "sent by God," in the original Greek of the New Testament, means to be dispatched from the very side of God to accomplish an assigned task. Can you imagine how much more peaceful you would be as a mother if you embraced that concept? You could stave off being overwhelmed by the three Cs (choice, comparisons, competition) in favor of beholding your child's Divine Assignment. One of the most shocking revelations any mother can have is that children are on loan. They don't belong to us. Our job is to help them understand the one who sent them, what they have been sent to do, and to whom they will return when their jobs are done.

Children as Windowpanes

Like freshly placed windowpanes that haven't been weathered or soiled by the environment, children can often see early what they perceive their purposes to be. After all, they haven't had as much input from well-meaning adults who are telling them what they ought to be. They speak from the heart. When my daughter, Madison, was two years old, she and I were lying on our tummies in the living room coloring. I asked her what she wanted to be when she grew up. Not thinking she would actually understand the question, I was shocked to hear her say, "A doggie doctor."

Similarly, my colleague Joan Malick used a wonderful technique when gathering material for a sermon. She asked questions of children, and she listened to their answers. She asked the kindergarten children and the fifth graders at our church if they had a sense of what God had sent them here to do. She gathered many answers, mostly in the form of professions. But one little person captured Joan's heart when he said, "I'm not quite sure what God has given me to do. But I do know that it will be good and I will be happy."

This child's comment is highly revealing for two reasons. First, it shows that children, who are more recently from the heart of God than adults, know instinctively that God's plan for them is good. They know that God's plan is for our joy in alignment with the gifts, interests, and passions God has placed in each of us. Second, this very insightful comment reveals how much we condition our children to think of themselves as not worthwhile until they have grown up. While Joan framed her question to potentially include the present, the child spoke of God's call on his life as something that would be revealed and implemented in the future! My fifth-grade daughter said, "I'm so tired of people asking me what I want to be when I grow up! Why can't I just be what I am now?" The happy mom understands that the time is now, and the child is present. She teaches him to look for ways today that he can fully live and express what God wants him to do and be even as a child. This discernment is not about God's rules and regulations; it's about the way that God wants this particular child to go as he lives out his Divine Assignment. Kids need to see that, like so many children in the Bible, they can make a difference right now. They don't have to wait to become a grownup to offer a significant contribution.

What if the little boy with the five loaves and two fish (John 6) had said to himself, "I need to wait until I grow up and graduate with a major before I offer this lunch because I'm only a little kid"?

Or where would we be if Samuel had ignored Eli's instructions to answer, "Speak, Lord, for your servant hears," just because he hadn't taken a vocational test to tell him if he was more suited to working with people or plastics (see 1 Samuel 3)?

How long would Naaman's life have been miserable with his skin disease if his nameless servant girl hadn't helped him find healing through the hand and words of Elisha (see 2 Kings 5)?

When we celebrate children for the difference they make in our lives and the lives of those around us, we let them know that we see traits and passions in them that make them significant because of who they are and not because of what they do. Just as the Divine Assignment we each have as a mother is first about who we are and not what we accomplish, children who grow up understanding this concept are much more able to live in the present, not always needing or wanting external things to make them happy or signal to them their importance.

Often we moms hold our breath because we aren't sure how our children are going to turn out. By giving kids the tools to articulate the difference they can make right now, we are helping them stay in a consistent cycle of self-discovery/application/affirmation about the place God calls them to be. They understand that one day feeds into the next as we grow and simply become instead of always feeling like we have to prepare for tomorrow.

So help your child get into the practice of articulating her vision by asking what impact she wants to make on the lives of others. Ask him to think about what he wants to be remembered for by his playmates, his schoolmates, and his family. Don't simply ask your children what they want to be when they grow up. This too often elicits the recitation of a profession they have heard others talk about. Listen to the threads in their visions for the near-term future and for their adult future, acknowledging their creativity in the process. Help them draw literal pictures and write word pictures describing what they see God calling them to do and be in the world.

Why Is It Hard to Behold?

Mothers face three particular challenges as we seek to implement the Beholding Lifesaver.

The first is that it's not always easy to let go of our children. We want to protect them from what others will think of them. We want to shelter them from making mistakes. We may even be concerned over what God is calling them to do. How do we learn to let go? One of the ways God reveals his purposes, intentions, and designs for humans is through the power of his natural creation. Mothering that aligns with God's loving design is a continuous cycle of nurture and release.

Pregnancy and birth is a powerful template of the ongoing rhythm of healthy motherhood. In pregnancy, there is time for nurture and time for release. If the cycle goes as intended, a baby emerges at just the right time, and everyone is healthy. While there is potential for a number of complications in any pregnancy, two are highly significant. If the nurture time is cut short for any reason, a premature baby is born posing challenges for the baby and the parents. If the baby won't emerge when a woman's body indicates it's time to come out, swift and decisive steps are taken to cause birth to eliminate danger to both the mother and the child.

We actually have very little control over when and how our baby is to be born. It's one of the unpredictable predictables we go through. We do, however, have great control of and responsibility for what happens in the following years. What if we took our cues from a God-given cycle?

When our children are babies we nurture much and release little, with the balance tipping more the older they get. But even babies are released to prevent harm. Imagine continuing to try to make a baby feed who is finished. Not pleasant. They need to be released!

As wise mothers not overcome by choice, comparisons, and competition, we can keep keen eyes on the cues our children give us for nurture and release. Each child is different, so it is absolutely futile for you to try to pick up nurture-and-release cues from what other mothers are saying about their kids. You may pick up a pointer or two regarding generalized temperament, but the beauty of the unfolding is only seen in your particular flower.

Second, this Beholding Lifesaver will never work if you are comparing your children to one another. One of the greatest gifts my parents gave to me and my sister was to recognize our very different talents and interests. Neither of us recalls a time when our parents said to either of us, "You should be more like your sister." Wise parents; noncompetitive children.

Last, we need to honestly admit that our children are not extensions of us. They are not put on earth for us to work out our own unlived lives and recessed dreams. We have been given our own lives to live. Whether we are doing that or not is not to infect what we expect our children to do or be.

Lori Wildenberg beautifully sums up the challenges we face to enjoy the distinctiveness of our children:

I've often wondered how Mary and Joseph felt after searching for their eldest son for three days, then finding him in the temple courts talking with the teachers. After the initial relief of locating Jesus, I wonder if they marveled at his growth. I wonder if they had that familiar parental pang in their chests.

Do you recall the first time you felt that tug on your heartstrings? I remember. My moment was eleven years ago. It still plays through my mind's eye. The vision is my oldest daughter crossing the street alone to go to the neighbor's home to play. Watching her every movement was bittersweet. Each step bringing her closer to her destination and farther away from me.

How does the unfolding of our children seem natural one minute, like a flower opening in the morning, yet so abrupt the next? With our first babies, we're so anxious for each developmental stage to be accomplished. Waiting with bated breath for the first words, first steps, first teeth.

Now I find myself dragging my feet. Resisting the inevitable—my child growing up. Rather than crossing the street on foot, my daughter is now at the brink of crossing the street behind the wheel. I'm aware another petal is unfolding.

Joseph and Mary's experience reminds me that my child is God's child first. She is here on this earth for a purpose, one that's separate from mine. She's meant to bloom. She won't always be with me but I pray that she'll flourish in her Father's house.

Respect and Honor

Two beautiful words describe the stance we need to take to deeply understand the fullness of what we are called to do as parents and stewards of the children God has given us to grow. These two sacraments unleash a sense of awe when we observe and interact with our children.

The first sacrament is to respect. While this takes some time, energy, and concentration, the pay-off is life changing. To respect someone means to look at him—really look at him—to see what he is truly all about. Not just what we think he's about or even what he was yesterday. To respect a child means we put down the dishcloth or the computer mouse, look into his eyes, and see what's really happened when we ask, "How was your day?"

When we ask what she sees for herself in the present and in the future, we need to truly listen and be reflective as she tells us. The more we respect, the more we accurately see and the clearer the path for our children as they are "trained in the way they should go." To respect children means to say to them, "I see who you are, and I believe it to be beautiful, worthwhile, and destined."

My husband, a marriage-and-family therapist, taught me a powerful tool to truly behold my children and others who cross my path. If we seek to honestly connect with other people, as they are unfolding a story or something that is troubling them, ask them during moments of silence, "Tell me more." The tone is inquisitive to give them open windows to express ideas and feelings that may be coming to the surface as they process information or an event.

After choir practice one Sunday morning, it was obvious that my daughter was agitated. She was bouncing off the walls—talking rapidly and unable to sit still. The more she talked, the more it became apparent that she was feeling invisible and unappreciated by some important people in her life, me included. As Madison started to cry and give me the list of things that had gone wrong in the past few days, I was highly tempted to give her reasons and excuses for the behavior of others to put things into perspective for her. But taking my cues from my wise husband, I said several times, "Tell me more." Once she had the chance to empty her feelings bucket and to realize that I was respecting her, she grew calm and was able to absorb the reasons her world was looking a little scary and unstable.

It's tempting, as mothers, to believe that we need to tell our children things in order for us to be fulfilling our job as parents. As Ginger Plowman, founder of Preparing the Way Ministries, observes,

> As parents, we often think that if we are able to verbalize our thoughts and feelings to our children, then we are good communicators. However, true communication is found not only in the ability to talk but also in the ability to listen. The art of successful communication involved not just expressing your thoughts and feelings but drawing out the thoughts and feelings of your children. In Proverbs 20:5, Solomon says, "The purposes of a man's heart are deep waters, but a man of understanding draws them out." Rather than talking "to" your children, learn to talk "with" your children.

The second sacrament is to honor. Once we respect our children, the next step is to honor them. Honoring is active, intentional, and overt.

In the Disney animated movie *Mulan* (1998), the title character defies her family and her entire culture to take her elderly father's place in war. She feels called or compelled to do this. As a woman, she is completely out of place. Early in the movie, she laments in song that she knows herself to be someone other than the cultural norm. She wonders when she will be recognized, beheld, and honored for her personhood.

She becomes a war hero, in part by mistake. Yet she is still female and feels tentative in her return home. What will her parents say, especially her father?

She takes him the spoils of war—a sword awarded to her by the emperor of Japan. As she presents the profound symbol to her father, he gives her an even greater gift. He beholds and honors her personhood as a woman of courage, dignity, beauty, and strength. He honors her essence and affirms her call. The changes in her approach and demeanor suggest she is transformed and completed by his recognition of her true self.

Honoring takes a lot of trust. We need to feel confident in our belief that God truly is in control of the life of our child, and that what is emerging in the vision is part of the plan. We need to embrace that society's expectations of our child may not fit who our child has been designed and created to be. It is a great step of faith to protect, nurture, and defend the dignity of the child's true call as we watch it unfold, without worrying about what the neighbors, teachers, or relatives think.

One of the greatest gifts you can give your children is true acceptance. You can help them mine the riches of their insides where their call and passion are waiting to be discovered and affirmed. This is what it means to respect and honor your child as you watch the unfolding. Not only does this enhance your child's concept of herself, it gives her the great gift of understanding and appreciating differences and diversity.

The Beholding Lifesaver proves immensely significant in the lives of mothers who have special-needs children. Christine came to me for coaching on her Divine Assignment because she was absolutely snowed under with the frustration of mothering her four-year-old daughter. Her daughter would not obey, fought Christine's every directive, ran away in stores, and treated her younger brother roughly, to the point that Christine was concerned for the safety of her baby. Christine was sure she was a terrible mother, and she certainly didn't feel she was living from her Divine Assignment.

Several weeks into our coaching sessions, Christine came into the office with her spirit obviously troubled. Through a series of tests, doctors and specialists had determined that her daughter had autism. In the course of our hour together, Christine began to see how this new information could be very helpful in giving her the tools she needed to use the Beholding Lifesaver to help herself stay sane. She understood that her child wasn't a bad child, and that she herself was not a bad mother. She understood that adjustments were going to need to be made that would actually bring more peace to her household based on the new, more accurate information about her daughter's wiring. Christine also realized she would need to let go of the temptation to believe her child was going to be like everyone else's, and to release the expectations of others on how her child "should" act and how Christine "should" mother. She could embrace that God had given her as a mother to her child and Christine had been given her daughter. Both of their Divine Assignments were in alignment with them being together.

The fascination of children is they are never finished. Day by day is a continual process of discovery and implementation. Whenever they express a piece of their vision, to honor them means to say, "Wow, I see that and I think that is fascinating." Honor means you look for the Spirit of God in the unfolding of your children, not what you think "should" be there.

The Beholding Lifesaver is a real sanity saver because it takes the pressure off you to make your child into something you think he should be and lets you enjoy the essence of who he really is. It helps you keep the focus of mothering where it really needs to be—on nurture and release. See what *is,* not what you want to see or what you wish was there. When you wholeheartedly respect and honor your children, you will deeply experience the joy and blessing of God's creation. In the rush to make sure your children have everything they need in life, don't leave the child behind.

Search and Rescue

1. *Warm up*—Which of the Central Passions would you use to describe each of your children? Respond to this quote by Albert Einstein: "Every child is born a genius."

2. What did you learn from your family of origin about honoring children?

3. What do you believe to be your child's greatest strengths?

4. Is your child turning out differently than you had hoped? Is this positive or negative for you?

5. Where are you in the cycle of nurture and release? Does one come more easily for you than the other? What would a good balance between the two look like for you?

6. Ask God what he is showing you through your children. Write out his answer.

7. *Assignment for the upcoming week*—Have your kids, if they are old enough, write their own personal definition of success, list five gifts and talents, and articulate a vision for when they have their first job. If they are not old enough, watch for personality traits and interests, write them down, keep them in a place you can refer to when they are older.

The Self-Care Lifesaver

Love the Lord your God with all your heart and
with all your soul and with all your mind
and with all your strength.

—JESUS OF NAZARETH (MARK 12:30)

Pull firmly on the mask, cover your nose and mouth, and breathe
normally. If you are traveling with children, please put your
mask on first before you assist them." Anyone who has ever flown
on a commercial airplane has heard this instruction from a flight
attendant regarding the proper use of the oxygen mask that tumbles
out of the ceiling in the event of unexpected loss of cabin pressure.
Early on, I thought it odd that parents would be instructed to put on
their masks first. Isn't the essence of parenthood to tend to your children first? Then I realized that if I am blue and laid out in the aisle
of the airplane, I won't do my children much good, no matter how
noble my intentions may be. And the same holds true in real life.

I knew I was in real trouble as a stay-at-home mom when I
would drop my kids off at a play date or preschool and drive along
the road for twenty minutes before I realized I was still listening to
Veggie Tales or the latest Disney soundtrack. I was losing myself
and not even knowing it. And I wasn't the only one.

A survey revealed that mothers feel they have made significant sacrifices. Seventy percent of moms questioned said being a mom is much more demanding and exhausting than they had expected. A whopping 86 percent feel moms don't get sufficient respect, and 80 percent responded that is particularly true for full-time moms. Nearly one quarter (24 percent) say they have lost their identity since they became mothers. The top sacrifices moms say they have made are privacy and quiet (57 percent), sleep (53 percent), carefree lifestyle (52 percent), self-indulgences (46 percent) and travel (36 percent).[1]

Professions Within the Profession

Apparently we're feeling a bit frazzled at times. And it's no wonder. When you consider all of the professions that are wrapped up in being a mom, it's a miracle any of us are still alive!

As Tutor, you are proficient at a wide variety of subjects including the foreign languages of toddlers and teenagers. You can switch from art class using cornstarch paint to science monitor overseeing the construction of a barometer using a baby food jar and a surgical glove.

As Doctor, you can take a temperature with the back of your hand on a forehead, handle tricky dispensing of a variety of medicines (crushed in applesauce), dispose of toxic bodily emissions, and have developed an impeccable and child-specific bedside manner.

And then there's Coach/Player. You can throw a ball, swing a variety of clubs and bats, wrestle, cheer from the sidelines, and handle all manners of winning and losing with appropriate congratulations and pep talks. And all of this doesn't even mention your weight-training prowess as you heft babies, groceries, furniture, and various diaper bags, book bags, backpacks, and totes!

As Therapist, you are well versed in the psychology of bedtime and the remarkable defense mechanisms used for not going to school. You understand the neurosis of having the toes in the socks just right before they go into the shoes, and the complex relationship of a third grader with her best friend.

Your role as Financial Planner finds you making decisions about who gets to eat this month and who doesn't. Not really, but you are consistently faced with replacing clothing, repetitive and frequent feedings using common (and cheap) ingredients, and deciding which utilities to pay first.

And let's not leave out the mainstays in our profession, Nutritionist and Chef. Notice I didn't say cook. Our culture prompts us to believe we need to be chefs and not just cooks! We read labels, balance carbohydrates and proteins, monitor servings, and do it all while cutting cute little things out of lunch meat to make an appealing and alluring presentation.

Your role as Mediation Specialist highlights your talents of separating children from other children, children from pets, and pets from other pets. You can break up a fist fight or a verbal barrage with equal dexterity. You have honed "now take turns" to optimized delivery.

As mothers, we have a lot going on.

Affirm Life

What is a Self-Care Lifesaver? The obvious answer is self-care is the opposite of self-abuse. When you aren't practicing self-care, you are practicing self-destruction. In a world where we are daily made aware of staggering violence, we need to be mindful to eliminate self-violence. Practice nonviolence with yourself first, and the healing effect spreads to others.

The less obvious answer is that self-care is actually the opposite of self-centeredness. Self-care is the God-given drive we have to protect life. Dallas Willard, in *The Divine Conspiracy,* illuminates why we feel compelled to take care of ourselves, to nurture ourselves.

> Unlike egotism, the drive to significance is a simple extension of the creative impulse of God that gave us being. We were built to count, as water is made to run down hill. We were placed in a specific context to count in ways no one else does. That is our destiny.
>
> Our hunger for significance is a signal of who we are and why we are here, and it also is the basis of humanity's enduring response to Jesus. For he always takes individual human beings as seriously as their shredded dignity demands, and he has the resources to carry through with his high estimate of them.[2]

God highly esteems you. That's the spiritual foundation of the Self-Care Lifesaver. Its core is choosing life. Its essence is choosing to affirm life—your life. Moses poses a disarmingly simple decision to his people in Deuteronomy 30:

> This day I call heaven and earth as witnesses against you that I have set before you life and death, blessings and curses. Now choose life, so that you and your children may live and that you may love the LORD your God, listen to his voice, and hold fast to him. For the LORD is your life..." (verses 19-20).

Choose life. This is an attitude as much as a behavior. There are some days when you honestly cannot squeeze any overt self-care into your schedule, but you can always choose life.

In their book *12 "Christian" Beliefs That Can Drive You Crazy*, Drs. Henry Cloud and John Townsend list this assumption at the top of the roster: "It's selfish to have my needs met." As licensed psychologists, they have observed their patients and note that "many of us have been taught a self-annihilation doctrine for so long that it makes sense to us. Yet to believe this is to confuse selfishness with stewardship. This crazy-making assumption—*'It's selfish to have my needs met'*—fails to distinguish between selfishness and a God-given responsibility to meet one's own needs. It's like someone saying, 'I saw you last night at the gas station, filling your car's tank. I had no idea you were so self-centered. You need to pray about spending more time filling others' tanks with that gas.' Yet if we don't fill our own tank with gas, we won't get far."[3]

So whether you put your own oxygen mask on first or fill up your own gas tank, the point is the same—you won't get very far or be truly helpful to those around you until you've attended to yourself first.

Jesus and the Balanced Life

So how do you choose life when you don't even have enough time to choose socks that match? In Mark 12:30, Jesus outlined what it means to be a whole person: "Love the Lord your God with all your heart and with all your soul and with all your mind and with all your strength." This is a comprehensive recipe for the balance we need in self-care.

Your "heart" is the seat of your will, attitudes, and intentions. In Old Testament Hebrew, the heart is the place where you make choices, and it's the deep pool of motives that define your decisions. While we may attribute our emotional life to the heart in contemporary terms, it is actually more about the will and on what foundation you base your life. This influential seat of power comes with a specific instruction: "Above all else, guard your heart, for it is the wellspring of life" (Proverbs 4:23). In other words, take good care of your heart and the rest of your life will be abundant.

Related to self-care, the first choice you make for life in your heart is to stay in uncluttered and consistent communication with the Holy Spirit. This is the wisest use of your will. From that powerful base, you can make all kinds of good decisions, including that of knowing and living your purpose. Drawing on your Divine Assignment, you can filter all of the other decisions you must make. You can cut through the things that don't fit for you and your family. You can stay on your path.

Your "soul" houses the part of you that knows there is something beyond yourself...that you are not alone. You choose life for your soul when you choose thoughts, attitudes, and expressions that bring you closer to God. You choose death for your soul when you engage in negative attitudes and behaviors that cause you to feel separated from God, from yourself, and from others. Many times when you feel lonely or experience legitimate guilt (very different from neurotic guilt), you have made a choice in thought, word, or deed that brings separation from God, self, or others.

Your intellect, mental health, and creativity camp in your "mind." This may be the easiest of the four (heart, soul, mind, strength) in which to choose life. Little choices made minute by minute such as watching television, listening to junk music, or engaging in gossiping rob you of self-care. Are you giving yourself care by what you watch or listen to? To whom you speak and what you say? You affirm life when you feed yourself nourishing input. You affirm life when you choose healthy food for your intellect and your creativity. You may not have uninterrupted time to enjoy an entire CD of your favorite music in a spa-like setting, but you do have the opportunity to practice self-care in what you listen to on a moment-by-moment basis throughout the day.

Your "strength" is your physical stamina and conditioning. When I wrote the book *The Proverbial Woman: Being a Wise Woman in a Wild World,* my intellectual uncle who is forever asking zany questions said, "How much do you think the proverbial woman weighs?" My reply was swift and certain, "She weighs as much as she needs to for maximum energy and attention to her purpose." Any more and you'll be bogged down. Obsession with any less and you will have a life cluttered with comparisons, unattainable goals, or just plain bad health from too much dieting and exercise. Strength and the body are simply tools—assets that are given to us to help us carry out our calls. Any excessive energy spent on them takes focus away from our true purpose.

Our strength also encompasses the fascinating intertwining of the mind and body. In order for us to have the desire to live life to the fullest, sometimes we have to address medical issues that have an impact on our emotional state. Anxiety and depression often have a physical root that must be addressed through medical attention and a good and proper prescription for the condition. If you have prolonged symptoms of anxiety or depression, or you have a family history of these conditions, consult a doctor you trust to help you correct any chemical imbalances. It's the same as if you had high blood pressure or diabetes. It's simply an issue of stewardship.

Make small choices for self-care everyday, such as choosing not to clean the macaroni and cheese off everyone's plate after lunch. Choose instead to eat an apple and drink a bottle of water. While we often think of self-care as the treats we give ourselves when no one else is around, true self-care is measured in the choices we make throughout our daily routine. In other words, if you don't have time for specific and identifiable self-care, are you simply going to give up and not take care of yourself? Or are you going to take a look at your daily routine and ask yourself where you could choose life more and choose death less?

My friend Jill is a weekday single mother. While her husband travels most of the week with his job, Jill is a full-time, stay-at-home mom for three adorable little girls. She has come up with a form of this Self-Care Lifesaver that she uses when she needs refreshment. She calls it the "All About Me Moment," or AAMM for short. Whenever she feels overboard, she says to herself, "AAMM," and reminds herself that she is important in this world and in the lives of her family members. She takes that moment to think about something nice she would like to do for herself, even if she can't in fact actually do it right then. Her little girls are getting to the developmental point where she now says, "I think I can take a bubble bath without anyone getting hurt."

What I appreciate about Jill's approach is this: She sees it as a moment-by-moment opportunity, realizing that it can't be a lifestyle right now. Her "All About Me" stance is not self-indulgent. It's a posture she takes so she can live her Divine Assignment and carry out her roles with maximum energy and joy. She doesn't beat herself up for being selfish, and she doesn't prolong the focus on herself. She's balanced.

Author and speaker Sherry Cummins encouraged mothers to do three things in her October 2002 article for *Hearts-at-Home Magazine:*

- Write down five things you enjoyed before you had children.

- Write down five things you would enjoy today if you have time.

- Write down five things you will enjoy when the kids are grown.

Sherry goes on to say,

> Today time is at a premium. In the hectic pace that you
> maintain, you have little time for the kids, let alone yourself.
> Have you put your life on hold until the children are grown?
> Somewhere along the line have you begun to feel resentful
> that you dedicated your energy toward the children and lost
> yourself? If you are waiting until you have more time, you
> have missed the point. Decide to begin your enjoyment
> journey now, to enjoy who you are and to share yourself with
> your children. Enrich them with your knowledge and expe-
> rience. You AND your children will reap the benefits. Don't
> wait for the destination—enjoy the journey.

Now, lest you think Sherry had lots of leisure time to pursue her
enjoyments, she was a single mother for most of the years her children were growing up. She speaks from authentic experience when
she encourages others to make time for themselves, and she is a
model that it can be done even as a single mother.

Why did Jesus say to love God with all our heart, soul, mind,
and strength? Is it because God is obsessed with our attention? Well,
yes, in a way. Not because it's good for God, but because it's good
for us. Self-care is not about shoulds and oughts. It's simply aligning
ourselves with the way we were created so we can be free and nour-
ished. It's not about what aligning with God does for God, it's about
what aligning with God does for us!

It's Still Hard

With this complete outline of what it means to practice self-care,
why is it still difficult to do it?

We are self-centered. By this I mean we are still worried about what other people are going to think. One mother asked, "Why do I feel so guilty when I just sit down for a few minutes and enjoy the quiet?" What will others think? Is my house clean enough? Are my children in enough activities? Do we do enough volunteer work so people will think we're good people? This type of self-centeredness seems to have other people as the focus, but it is still centered around self and the impression self is making in our society focused on comparison and competition.

We are out of partnership with God. At lunch with a woman who was very dedicated to her job, I was struck by the remarkable power we often attribute to other people whom we believe can ultimately influence our future. She was bothered by the choice she felt she had to make between showing integrity in her current job and the effect that might have on the recommendations she would receive from her employer when the time came for her to make a job change. We often believe people hold the key to our next promotion, where our children are going to go to college, how much money we make, or what kind of opportunities will come our way. As she outlined what these people could do to her, I stopped her mid-sentence and asked, "Hey, who's in charge here?" At first blush, the self-improvement movement has trained us to say, "I am." The answer behind the answer for those who know God is "God is." It is our partnership with God that brings our present and our future to be. God makes all paths straight as we trust. So we don't need to over-function to engineer or secure our future.

We're tired. Truthfully, there are times in the normal cycle of being female that we are simply tired, physically depleted by our hormonal dictatorship. Self-care, the Lifesaver that could best minister to us at that point, is the option we tend to choose last! We turn to stimulants such as soda or opiates such as television. These are the times to ask more than ever, "What will it mean for me to choose life?" Healthy practices are based on consistent, intentional behavior and attitude, not on whether we feel like it or not.

Depression strikes. A lack of interest in self-care may also be an indicator of something more than ten million people of our country suffer from, but it is still a topic that is kept under wraps. Clinical depression, based on a chemical imbalance, drags thousands of women into the chilly waters of being overwhelmed and disinterested in taking care of themselves. At one point in my life, even before I became a mother, I went to a doctor for my PMS. He asked how many days a month I had PMS, and I told him 13 to 15. He gently said to me, "Robin, that's not PMS. You are clinically depressed." With his care, a wise understanding of my depression as having physical roots, and a wonderful medication, I came back from a life that had been marked by tears, anxiety, guilt, and lethargy—even though no one else knew! As a primary point of self-care, be sure you are getting regular physicals with a doctor who listens to you and works well with you.

What should you do to use the Self-Care Lifesaver? This is revealed through your dynamic, personal, and consistent interaction with the Holy Spirit. You and the Spirit will figure out your authentic temperament and choose Lifesavers for heart, soul, mind, and strength that speak to your particular life. Here's a hint: Revisit your Divine Assignment, and ask God to show you what practices of self-care will help you more fully live your purpose.

Choice, Not Time

Self-care has more to do with choice than time. It takes the same amount of time to drink a soda as it does to drink a bottle of water.

In the time you spend showering, you can choose to use products that bring you joy. In the time we take to talk with a friend, what do we choose to say? Same amount of time spent. We make significant choices in life or death simply by what we choose to talk about.

Sometimes you can't actually do much in a day that looks like self-care, but you can always ask yourself, "Am I choosing life?" In this practice, as with the others, we are teaching our children what it means to be an adult by the way we interact with life. When you choose to affirm your own life by practicing self-care, you are teaching your children that God treasures all of us, so we treasure ourselves. You teach them that it's a good thing to be grown-up. You model for them that being a parent is not a task that destroys the self. The Self-Care Lifesaver that you embrace will have far-reaching effects through generations of your family. You teach your children responsibility because, by the very definition of self-care, you are the only one who can do it. You will begin to produce people who can love their neighbors because they love themselves.

And, hey, don't be afraid to let your kids listen to *your* music. The jazz, gospel, classical, or soft rock might actually be good for them!

Search and Rescue

1. *Warm up*—What is your favorite way to rejuvenate yourself?

2. What is your perspective on self-care?

3. How do you respond to the idea that it is imperative that we put ourselves first? How is that overdone in our culture? How is it underdone in our culture? What are the consequences of either position?

4. Write the answers to the three suggestions Sherry Cummins gave in this chapter:

    a. Write down five things you enjoyed before you had children. *—travelling —reading —exercising —going to movies by myself*

    b. Write down five things you would enjoy today if you have time. *—travelling —reading —exercising —going to movies*

    c. Write down five things you will enjoy when the kids are grown. *—travelling —going to movies —reading —exercising*

5. Given Jesus' outline of a balanced life, what do you need to do to take better care of your:

    a. heart   c. mind

    b. soul *pray more*   d. strength

6. Ask God why you should put your own oxygen mask on first. Write out his answer.

7. *Assignment for the upcoming week*—On purpose, leave something undone that you think you "ought" to do in favor of doing something nourishing for yourself. Note your responses and feelings about this.

8

The Listening Lifesaver

He who listens, understands.

—AFRICAN PROVERB

The first duty of love is to listen.

—PAUL TILLICH

My husband and I were moving into our first "real" house, and I was so excited! We had been living in a really cute little townhome, but it was time to get a house that had at least two more bedrooms than we could sleep in, a kitchen where I could actually talk to guests while preparing appetizers, enough living space so that I didn't have to watch TV if I didn't want to, and David didn't have to be quiet so I could read if he didn't want to. This was thrilling!

I was so excited that I was moving at a rapid pace to close up the townhome and get on with my new life in my new home. You know how those last few boxes go—just throw anything in them, just get everything cleared out. Not wanting to pack dirty dishes, I decided to run one more load through the dishwasher. Oops, the dishwasher soap was already packed, and I was not going to go to the store just for a box of that stuff. Hmm, what do we have here? Okay, there's a bottle of dishwashing soap. That ought to work.

During the first cycle, I learned why dishwasher manufacturers want you to use dish soap designed especially for dishwashers. There is a reason why some dish soap is for the sink and some of it is for the machines. Big, billowing clouds of soapsuds rapidly grew out around the door of the dishwasher and even up through the pipes into the sink as the large amounts of water poured into the machine met the large amount of liquid soap meant for the sink. As I frantically opened the door interrupting the cycle, I realized I was going to be there a while scooping billions of soap bubbles. I was going to have to get dishwashing soap anyway, now on top of taking care of the chaos I had created. If only I hadn't been in such a hurry. And now I was also going to be totally embarrassed when my husband found out what I had done.

I didn't "listen" to the machine manufacturer, and I made a huge mess. While this error was rather comical when all was said and done, the truth remains that we need to listen to those who are wiser than we are, and we need to pursue good input in order to keep from getting messy output.

As you are beholding and honoring your children, you already know the power of truly listening. This Lifesaver can be very fruitfully extended to include others in your life as you seek to be a mother who swims, not sinks.

The Most Powerful Listening Tool

I credit my husband, a therapist, for helping me be as well-adjusted as I am today. (He says he doesn't want to take the blame!) David has taught me some wonderful tools over the years for improving my relationships with people and with myself. One potent listening tool is called "Is there anything else?"

In order to truly listen, we must be willing to suspend and quiet the constant chatter that rattles in our brains. In order to truly listen, we must be willing to focus on and absorb what the other person is saying. Mostly because we are quite busy and rushed, we are prone to quick fixes and answers that reflect our need to make things better within the time it takes to get a cheeseburger, ketchup only, from a fast-food drive-through.

This is how the "Is there anything else" works. Imagine yourself in several different conversations. The first is with your seven-year-old, who is inconsolable because he has lost yet another chess match to his father, who beats him every time. Your son has gone off to bed wailing that he is a loser and a freak. A strong maternal tendency is to go into the room with the intent of bolstering his ego, telling him all the reasons he is a great little guy and making him feel better with words of comfort and encouragement.

What if, instead, you sat with him while he's crying and asked him how he was feeling? He sobs, "I'm such a little idiot!"

You ask, "Is there anything else? How else are you feeling?"

He cries, "I'll never win at chess!"

You continue, "Is there anything else?" And on this goes until he has exhausted his self-deprecating arsenal.

This happened in our house and within minutes my son and I were sitting on his bed eating bowls of cereal, with him smiling and chatting. A few minutes into our feast, sort of off-the-cuff, I asked, "You don't really think you're a loser, do you?" He grinned that funny little grin that kids do when they know they've been goofy. That's all the answer he needed to give me.

Or imagine you're in a more heated conversation with someone who feels, at that particular moment, like an enemy. Say it's time to balance the checkbook, and there are some missing entries. Your husband says, "I really wish you would be organized enough to enter your purchases when you make them." Now stick with me here as we go through this process. Get your blood pressure back under control.

In a tone that is inquisitive but not defensive, you ask, "I can see how that would be frustrating. Is there anything else?"

"Yes," he says. "I'm nervous when I see holes in the checkbook that don't match with the bank statement. I feel like our finances are out of control when that happens."

Again, inquisitive not defensive (you may want to practice ahead of time), you ask, "Is there anything else?"

"Yes," he says. "I don't like the way I feel about us when I'm worried about money."

Here you can use a variation on the theme. "Say more about that."

Well, pretty soon you've uncovered that this man really misses you and the fun you used to have together as a couple before all of the responsibilities came into your lives. You learn that he is lonely without you, feels a great deal of pressure to provide, and wants to take you to the Bahamas for a two-week romp on the beach (okay, it may not go that far). But by keeping your cool and really listening, you have defused a potential powder keg and have learned something more about this special man to whom you are married.

And, yes, this takes time. That's why it's counted among the Lifesavers. Lifesavers are often practices that cause us to buck the societal flow—or should I say gush—and enable us to live life more in God-time. God-time is whatever time you need to be peaceful, grounded, and connected. Any other pace is not healthy, and you will feel like you are drowning.

One of my favorite blessings in using this tool is that it takes me off the hook of having to be the answer woman. Sometimes I get so caught up in being smart that I forget to be wise. Smart means I have the answer; wise means I provide the space for the answer to emerge.

I have noticed it's almost always more wise to let someone come up with his or her own conclusion than for me to provide one.

As I teach this "Is there anything else" tool, I can see the anxiety rising in some of my clients. They ask:

◯ What if I don't have time for this?

◯ What if they never stop?

◯ What if I never get a chance to say my piece or defend myself?

◯ What if they don't come to the "right" conclusion?

Most of the time the clients haven't actually tried to use the tool and haven't seen the power of the process. So I encourage them, as I encourage you, to give this tool a try and discover the potency of the paradox. It's an issue of trust.

Listening to the Holy Spirit

The Holy Spirit speaks to us in many ways, but the result is always the same. We are energized, soothed, encouraged, and enlightened by the still, small voice that plays in our hearts at various times.

My favorite way to view my relationship with the Holy Spirit is to imagine myself as a radio receiver. Radio sound waves are constantly running through the air, just waiting for a receiver to have its dial tuned to the right station for the radio waves to be turned into sound that soothes, educates, entertains, or energizes the listener. I need to realize that the Holy Spirit is always around me and inside of me. I can best listen when my dials are rightly set and I'm picking up the transmissions that God is constantly sending.

As my friend Laurie Beth Jones says, "Try to make sure the still small voice doesn't stay still or small."

Listening to Wise Counsel

Some of the best people to listen to are people who are themselves good listeners. These are wise and loving people in your life who deeply listen to what you have to say and can lead you to your own water to drink. Proverbs 20:5 says, "The purposes of a man's heart are deep waters, but a man of understanding draws them out." Have you ever had something on your mind or a challenge you needed to face? Did you have the opportunity to talk about it with someone? If you left the conversation saying, "She is so wise," chances are good that she listened, asked questions, and helped you draw your own conclusions about your situation. Each of us holds a rich well of wisdom in our own hearts and souls. It's the Holy Spirit living in us. But sometimes it takes conversation with another sensitive and listening person to draw the water out of us that we might not have been able to draw ourselves. The wisest people I know are the ones who are good listeners.

These people in our community who are wise, loving, and good listeners themselves can become part of our wisdom council. Throughout Proverbs, we are shown the desirability of having wise people to turn to. Their teachings are a fountain of life (13:14), they will help us grow wise as we walk with them (13:20), they spread knowledge (15:7), they give good and thoughtful answers (15:28), and they are discerning (16:21). Wouldn't you like to have some people in your life who are like this? Proverbs tells us, "He who gets wisdom loves his own soul; he who cherishes understanding prospers" (19:8), and "listen to advice and accept instruction, and in the end you will be wise" (19:20). Ask God to begin to show you who these people are in your life. And ask him to bring you others who can become part of your wisdom council.

Listening to Our Kids

When it comes to listening to our kids, this is the perfect time to highlight the difference between hearing and listening. To stay afloat as a mother, you need to know that you don't have to attend to every little noise that comes from your children! If they are anything like my children, you'll hear them continually. The secret to sanity is to know two critical distinctions.

The first is that hearing is constant, and listening is focused. For mothers with typical auditory abilities, hearing is a continuous function. It's not optional. Listening, on the other hand, is focused as we choose to attend to what we're hearing. You may have heard or used the phrase "perked up my ears." That means there may be a lot of noise going on in the backseat of your van that you don't pay attention to, but if you hear a certain phrase or it becomes apparent you need to settle something, you turn your focus to really listening. Just knowing this difference can set you back on the deck of the S.S. Sanity in short order. As a mother and a person with her own brain, set yourself free from the notion that you have to focus on every word your kids speak.

Second, hearing is passive, and listening is active. Listening means I will not only focus on what I'm hearing, I will turn my attention to thoughtfully respond to what I'm hearing. For example, my kids chatter. They sometimes talk utter nonsense just to hear themselves talk. If I thought I had to actively engage with every sound they make, I would be agitated and definitely in the water trying to keep up with the sheer amount of input. But I can let my hearing be passive until I get a cue that I need to actively engage in listening. Everything they say does not necessitate a response on my part.

I am not, of course, advocating that we ignore our children. When they truly need to tell us something and receive a caring and helpful response, or have us celebrate or commiserate with them, we are there. As mothers, we know from our instincts, or because a child just flat out says "You're not listening to me!" that it's time to be focused and active in listening.

It Takes Time

As we look back over the Listening Lifesaver, one thing is abundantly clear—it takes time. If we are too busy to listen, we are just plain too busy. If we are running out the door to take Junior to another sports practice in hopes that being on a winning team will improve his self-esteem, we might be better off improving his self-esteem by simply sitting and listening to him, honoring him, letting him know another human being deeply cares about him. If we are headed off to another project, class, benevolence, or event because there is a void inside that is seeking connection, we might consider spending that same time connecting with ourselves, our God, or others in our wisdom council. Whether you are an extrovert who needs to connect with other people for your energy source or an introvert who needs to connect with the Holy Spirit and yourself for rejuvenation, the supply of your vigor comes from true listening. That's where the life-giving connection originates.

Search and Rescue

1. *Warm up*—Sit completely still for one minute.

2. Describe a time when you felt someone truly listened to you. Who was it, and how did it make you feel?

3. What did you learn about listening to children from your own childhood? What did you learn about listening to significant others? What did you learn about listening to society?

4. To whom do you listen? Are you stronger or weaker for listening to their input?

5. Who is in your wisdom council and why?

6. Ponder Psalm 5:3: "In the morning, O LORD, you hear my voice; in the morning I lay my requests before you and wait in expectation." What does that mean for you at the present time? We may be good at laying out our requests, but how do we wait in expectation? Discuss some ways you might genuinely do this and what might need to be altered in your life for you to hear God's voice.

7. Ask God to whom you need to be listening more carefully. Write out his answer.

8. *Assignment for the upcoming week*—Practice "Is there anything else?" on three people. What kind of conversation did you end up having with each of them?

The Laughter Lifesaver

If you can roll with the punches and laugh when you
could just as easily get angry, it will be to your
advantage 100 percent of the time.

—ZIG ZIGLAR

To sail in laughter is to live in a state of grace. Sometimes laughter comes easily, sometimes we have to work at it a little. Sometimes laughter erupts from us in spite of our tears or anger. True laughter is always a gift, and gifts are always of grace.

Is there anything so wonderful as the sound of people you love laughing? When it's your kids in the backseat, it can be so raucous and irritating. Yet it beats the sound of bickering anytime. And what can surpass the feeling you have when you are laughing so hard that you can hardly breathe, tears are running down your face, and you are completely in synch in that particular moment in time because you are totally lost in laughter? Have you ever paid attention to how you feel after that? Many times the feeling right after a good laugh is "Whew, I'm tired but peaceful." Or you may wonder what it was that was bothering you a few minutes ago. Or you may have discovered new resolve to tackle a problem or obstacle that has been facing you and your family.

The Laughing Role Model

As mothers, we are powerful role models for our children as they watch us and learn from us what's funny and what isn't. They learn how to handle humorous and tense situations alike by watching our reactions. Our children take potent cues from us about appropriateness and coping, respect and self-confidence. All of these lessons come to them by observing what makes Mommy and Daddy laugh.

Laughter highlights our priorities. When we can laugh instead of yell, we give our children the freedom to make mistakes, to be themselves, and to know that, although they may indeed be in trouble, home is going to be characterized by humor and not by humiliation.

Author and speaker Lynn Shaw relates that laughter has absolutely saved her countless times as a mom. She had two baby boys in two years and found the demands of working full-time outside of the home, being involved in her church and community, and caring for two babies frequently overwhelming. She ruefully admitted that she found herself yelling in the first two years of motherhood and would immediately regret the harsh tone of her spoken words as her two little ones would flinch. Lynn not only set her personal desires to cope differently with her tiredness and frustrations, she accessed her professional skills as a social worker and decided an intervention was needed.

One Saturday morning, Lynn was sorting through the one-too-many piles of clothes and loading the washer. Already having heard the "mommy, mommy, mommy" mantra several times that morning, she felt the tension rising as one more time her boys ran to her yelling, "Mommy!" Just as the boys arrived near the laundry, Lynn stuck her head inside the washing machine and yelled, "A,B,C,D,E,F,G..." until she got all the way to Z! Pulling her head out of the machine, she looked at her two boys to find two pairs of wide eyes. Her two-year-old turned to his one-year-old brother and exclaimed, "Mommy knows her ABCs!" Lynn laughed out loud, and the two boys smiled and laughed with her.

Laughter also has other benefits to us as mothers. When we use laughter as we are teaching our children, we connect with our children by disarming them. Educators and entertainers of all kinds know that if you can get your audience to laugh, you have increased your chances of your message sticking. Often we believe we must be stern for a child to remember a lesson. Depending on the gravity of the offense, this may be true. However, what if we decided that for the everyday recurring offenses we endure, we were going to make our point while laughing? We may find that our point is more favorably received, and our blood pressure is certainly lower.

We shape behavior by what we laugh at. How many times have you been at the dinner table and had a child do something spontaneously funny? When you laugh at them and say, "Oh, that was so funny," what do you find happening in the next instant? He is reenacting the behavior. Children instinctively know that glee-filled laugher is a good thing, and they want to have as much of it in their lives as possible.

Laughter Is Good Medicine

Laughter is, in fact, a wonderful healer. Although the writers of the book of Proverbs didn't have access to all of the sophisticated medical knowledge we have today, someone still penned this wisdom thousands of years ago: "A cheerful heart is good medicine" (17:22). Laughter awakens endorphins, eases muscle tension, stimulates the heart and respiratory rate, increases circulation, and exercises stomach and chest muscles. Physicians report a few minutes of deep belly laughing is the equivalent of a few minutes of exercise on a rowing machine. A hearty chuckle boosts your immune system by increasing levels of activated T cells, immunoglobulins, and B cells, which are necessary in healing and fighting disease. Laughter decreases the levels of so-called "stress hormones" in the body that may cause ulcers, high blood pressure, and headaches. Interferon-gamma, fighter of viruses and parasites, increases significantly during and after laughter. As Max Eastman says, "Laughter puts your brain, your central nervous system, and your whole being into a state of free play."

Laughter does all that and more in healing our souls. God surprises us at times with opportunities for laughter when we fear we are reaching the end of the tether and won't be able to tie a knot. When we can laugh through our tears, we discover a powerful truth: Things may be bad, but they aren't completely and eternally bad. It's the laughter that takes us off guard that shows us the truly gracious nature of God.

Rhonda is a wonderful example of a mother who has chosen laughter over anger. Do you see your own household in any of her stories?

For the first five years of motherhood, I was blessed to have an angelic son named Joey, who never had behavior problems. He was quiet, gentle, easygoing, and obeyed instantly. Actually, he didn't need to obey because he almost always knew how to behave. Other mothers would look at me and shoot poison arrows from their eyes. My sweet little boy was the envy of all mothers. My husband and I congratulated ourselves, not knowing exactly what we were doing right, but nevertheless, smugly accepting all accolades and praises that were heaped upon us.

Then I had Cullen.

Even at ten days old, I knew Cullen was different from Joey. As an infant, Joey could sleep five hours straight in the middle of the afternoon. Cullen took cat naps all day, and when he was awake, his eyes were as big as saucers, taking it all in. Little did I know, those big eyes were casing the joint, plotting for the day he would eventually walk.

Cullen learned to walk at 13 months old, and the house was never quite the same after that. He was strong-willed, independent, and extremely self-sufficient. When he learned to walk, I was four months pregnant, which is not exactly the best time to chase a toddler on the brink of discovery. He exhausted me. My husband, who worked during the day and was a college student by night, could not be there with me for those long evenings at home after I had already put in a full day at the office. It was just the three of us—me, Joey, and Cullen. I began to dread the evenings after work, so much so that I would cry in the office parking garage before picking up Cullen from daycare. I would pray, "Lord, please give me the energy to get through this pregnancy, to love my sons, and to try and enjoy Cullen's babyhood," since I knew that his time as the baby of the family would abruptly end in March, when our third baby was scheduled for delivery.

God did not choose to make my life easier by giving Cullen a docile and compliant spirit. Instead, God chose to work on *my* spirit. One night after picking up Joey from after-school care, I struggled to get Cullen into his car seat. He had such disdain for his car seat. He would arch his back and stiffen his body so that I could not, no matter how hard I tried, conform his body to a sitting position. At 30 pounds, Cullen was no lightweight, and he was strong. I may as well have been trying to restrain a mule. I was leaning on the car door in tears, five months pregnant, and rain was drizzling down in 40-degree weather. It was late, and I was tired and hungry. I glanced at my defiant little boy and burst into laughter. I was laughing and struggling with Cullen and the car seat at the same time. The more I struggled, the harder I laughed. I laughed so hard that it hurt. It could only have been the Lord who caused my fit of laughter that night in the cold and rain.

As the days went by and the pregnancy limited my energy, Cullen got older and his capacity for getting into trouble increased. One day, when he was hungry, he went to the refrigerator and brought me the food that he wanted—a whole rotisserie chicken that he held by one leg, the congealed chicken fat dripping all over my carpet. It slipped from his grip and thumped to the carpet in a heap of chicken fat, splattering on all that was in its vicinity. It was a laugh or cry moment. I chose to laugh and wondered if Heloise knew how to get the chicken smell out of carpet.

Another morning right before we left the house for daycare, I found Cullen with a red marker. Large, jagged bolts of red marker shot up from his bare legs and feet. His face looked jaundiced. As I examined him more closely, his cheeks and forehead were slathered in yellow marker. As if on instinct, I went to his crib. The wall beside his crib was yellow, and his crib sheet was yellow and red. He had taken markers to bed with him the night before, squirreling them away before bed so I didn't notice them. "No wonder he never cried to be picked up this morning," I reasoned. He had been too busy. I was late for work, and the marker was not washable. All I could do was laugh and pick him up for a hug. He went to daycare looking that way. When we arrived at school, Cullen's teachers did not see the humor in it as I did, but I think they felt pity for me. "That's okay," I thought. "They don't know that this was Divine Laughter coming from me, that Jesus was loving Cullen through me."

Eventually, March rolled around and our daughter, Katie, was born. There were dark days ahead while I tried to care for a newborn and lasso Cullen at the same time. But through it all I managed to keep a sense of humor about myself, and when times got tough, I threw my back my head and laughed. Sometimes it was laughter through tears, and sometimes tears came simply because I was laughing so hard at my children and their antics.

Almost a year later, Cullen is slowly coming out of his difficult stage, and God remains in His heaven, laughing right alongside me, just when I need to hear Him. The Book of Proverbs tells us there is virtue in a woman being able to laugh. I can attest to that. Just as no one should cry over spilt milk, we shouldn't shed a tear over congealed chicken fat either.

"Not Tonight, Dear..."

One of the most common losses in the lives of married couples when they become parents is the physical intimacy they had before the children arrived. Once plentiful resources like time, energy, attention, and opportunity seem to evaporate, and sex just isn't what it used to be.

Entire books are written on the subject of addressing this frustration in this developmental phase of a family, so I won't play sex therapist at this point. I'll simply offer a different perspective.

Rather than lament over your love life, find ways to enhance your laugh life. While you may not have the energy or desire or opportunity to frequently engage each other sexually, you may be able to find time to pop a funny DVD into the machine and enjoy a good laugh together. You may want to keep a collection of movies the two of you enjoyed before you had children. Show each other funny comics from the paper. Tell each other goofy things you saw during the day. Laughing together can ease tensions and reconnect you, even with your clothes on and in the presence of the children. Shared laughter can be shared intimacy.

Imperfect Laughter

By modeling laughter for our children, we teach them to keep things in perspective. One major obstacle to laughter is perfectionism. We have a difficult time laughing when we are angry over something not being "right." God's grace comes to us through laughter as we realize there is no perfection on earth, and to expect that to be the standard is setting everyone up for disappointment. When something doesn't go right, we need to learn to not take it so personally. I am not advocating a lack of personal responsibility, but many of us seem to think there is more in our control than there actually is. Truly healthy laughter at ourselves helps our children be more adventurous themselves. They learn that making mistakes is human, and they are loved anyway.

When deciding between the practice of laughter and the practice of perfectionism, noted child psychologist and family expert T. Berry Brazelton suggests we ask ourselves on a regular basis, "Why is this so important to me?" When we don't feel like laughing, or we are just plain angry at our children's behavior or another irritant, it can be a signal that something important is being violated. A norm from our own family of origin may be at risk or a cultural expectation may not be met. When that little voice inside says "You really can laugh at this" but you still feel hesitant, wondering if you will give the wrong message in your laughter, discern if it's really a deeply held belief of your own or a response to the external comparisons and competition that seek to steal your joy. After all, who among us has not felt like laughing with our children when everything around them is serious and something strikes them funny?

Why Is She Laughing?

You will be amazed how much more laughter will come naturally when you are freed from the three choppy Cs. One of the most famous "laughers" in the Old Testament is found in the last chapter of the book of Proverbs. The woman of Proverbs 31 was noted because "she can laugh at the days to come" (verse 25). Where does laughter come from? A heart that is free. True laughter comes from a soul that is prepared. She has identified her Divine Assignment and is working from that soul name in all she does. This affects her relationships, finances, organization, physical health, and options for involvement. She can laugh because she's carefree. She can laugh because she is sure of her choices, free from comparisons, and doesn't give in to the violence of competition. Why can she laugh? She knows who she is and that she's in God's abundant care. She has done what Lady Wisdom in the book of Proverbs tells her to do, "First pay attention to me, and then relax. Now you can take it easy—you're in good hands" (1:31 THE MESSAGE).

What's So Funny?

Happy moms love to laugh at all kinds of things. Funny movies, the giggling of their own children, and the way their kids see the world. Libby observes, "Jokes told wrong by kids are funnier than jokes told right by adults!"

Karen loves to watch her daughter play with the family pets. "Abby plays tag and pretend football with our two Bichon dogs. It's as if the dogs really communicate with Abby. They all seem like they are having so much fun as they take turns being 'it.' For football, they seem to know what the imaginary goal line is. It's a hoot."

One mother even observed, "I think it's funny that you're asking my opinions and experiences for a book!"

In our family, we seem to get the biggest laughs out of our stream-of-consciousness conversations while we're together eating or traveling in the van. One early autumn day we were driving through the hills of southern Indiana enjoying the pumpkin patches, observing the newly changing colors on the trees, and anticipating meeting our friends for a day of outdoor play on their farm. Earlier in the year, we had traveled to Gatlinburg, Tennessee, for spring break. I commented as we rolled through the hills past the enchanting streams running through the roadside forests, "This reminds me of Gatlinburg." That's when it started.

My children, neither of them given to silence, took the opportunity to skip down the path of remembering laced with word play. Madison began her travelogue welcome to the national park near Gatlinburg. Her younger brother Grant tried to join in, but in his excitement tripped over the name.

"Welcome to Gag…Gag… What's it called Burg?"

Before my husband or I could even give him the correct name, Madison hollered, "Welcome to Gagmewithabird!" I thought we were going to have to pull over, we were laughing so hard. The initial laughter of being stunned with such an absurd thought became more intense as we laughed at the fact that we were laughing, then laughed because it was just so much fun to hear each other laughing so hard.

That story exemplifies an important principle in this Laughter Lifesaver. You may read the account and think we're crazy. "What's so funny about that?" The point is, laughter comes to different families in different ways. Most often it isn't planned, and even more often it is personalized to your particular family, the places you've been, the things you have seen, and the bonds you share because of these commonalities.

Don't Laugh Now!

It can be challenging to know when to laugh and when not to laugh. Jennifer told me of her quandary one day as her very serious daughter came scowling into the house through the laundry room door adjacent to the garage door. Jennifer asked her daughter, "What's wrong?"

"It's my little brother. He's embarrassing me."

"How is he doing that?" Jennifer asked.

"Go out and look," came the reply. Her daughter disappeared down the hall and closed her bedroom door.

Jennifer went outside. Larger than life, there was a hearty and healthy three-year-old boy riding his tricycle in circles on the driveway. What distinguished him, and embarrassed his sister, was that he was attired only in a red fireman's hat and yellow rain boots. Jennifer was indeed caught. She thought the antics were hysterical, yet she wanted to be sensitive to her daughter's mortification over the display. What would you do?

Of course, there are times when we truly do not laugh. When stern discipline really is necessary, keep laughter at bay to keep the boundaries clear between things that can be dealt with in a humorous way and things that can't. No laughing when someone is truly hurt or if it will hurt someone's feelings. Don't laugh when tensions are too high because it can add fuel to the fire. As my mother always said, "Timing is everything."

And there is a gigantic difference between laughing *with* our children and laughing *at* our children. When practicing laughter, seek to laugh *together* about things that are funny. Izzy Gesell observed, "Shared laughter is love made audible." Children feel included when we laugh with them. They feel excluded when we laugh at them. On the rare occasion when we must laugh at them because their pouting or tantrum is so funny, draw them close and help them see the situation from your perspective, perhaps even reenacting their behavior. Often that diffuses an angry standoff. Laughing at our children without inviting them into our circle of laughter is one sure way to frustrate them. The trick is letting the child know how much you value him, even if you're making a parental point by poking fun. We can teach our children to laugh at themselves in a loving way, and to laugh with others in an inclusive way. How do we best teach this kind of laughter? By being the laughing role model.

Joyful Noise

If H.L. Mencken is right and "God is a comedian whose audience is afraid to laugh," the Laughter Lifesaver will help dispel the fears and bring refreshment and renewed perspective to our lives. While we often think of singing when hearing the psalmist's invitation to "make a joyful noise," we could just as easily include the glee of giggles. Sail in the gift of laughter and live in a state of grace.

Search and Rescue

1. *Warm up*—What is the funniest scene you've ever seen in a movie?

2. What makes you laugh?

3. What makes your family laugh? Share or write about a time when your family was consumed in laughter.

4. How would you respond to a situation where one child thinks something is funny and one child doesn't?

5. What are you teaching your children by what you laugh at?

6. What is the difference between laughing at and laughing with? How do you think it affects children?

7. Ask God what makes him laugh. Write out his answer.

8. *Assignment for the upcoming week*—A University of Michigan study reveals that kids laugh 150 times a day, but adults only 15. Laughing 150 times a day reduces stress and equals the effect of 15 minutes on a stationary bike. This week concentrate on laughing, and see how many times a day you really do laugh.

10

The Play Lifesaver

Play keeps us vital and alive. It gives us an
enthusiasm for life that is irreplaceable. Without it,
life just doesn't taste good.

—Lucia Capacchione

In Indianapolis, Indiana, on May 15, 2002, a 43-year-old grand-father punched a peewee team baseball coach four times, after screaming profanities at the coach's wife. The coach's transgression? He changed the batting order, ultimately causing his team to lose the game. Witnesses to the scene were boys and girls ages 5 to 8.

A University of Michigan study reported that 70 percent of the 2 million American kids who participate in organized sports will give up playing by the time they are 13.[1] The reason? The behavior of grown-ups is taking the fun out of it.

A newspaper story entitled "Bringing Up Baby" sports the sub-title "Parents look for ways to give their little ones a developmental edge at a younger age."

Even the Girl Scouts of America recognizes the enormous pres-sure our kids are under. The scouts have launched the new "Stress Less" badge "designed to help girls cope with the pressure-cooker conditions confronting even young children today."

What in the world is going on here? Adults have forgotten how to play, and we're infecting the young with the disease.

Some Play...

Some mothers find it easy to play. They don't feel guilty or hesitant about it at all. By nature or temperament, they can set aside the cultural expectations of their daily lives leaving time to romp, read books, and relax. Gary Trent and John Smalley have a wonderful description of this personality type in their book *The Two Sides of Love*. They call these carefree people "otters," and their very motto in life is "Let's play!"

Some Don't...

But for the rest of mothers who find it difficult to play, the issues are often related to upbringing or inborn temperament. These are some common hesitations to play.

1. *The work has to get done first.* Many of us weren't raised to play. We were told that we had to finish our work before we could do anything else. That was fine as children. Delayed gratification is an important skill to learn as it keeps us from being irresponsible about important issues and tasks. But as we grew into adults, with increased demands and responsibilities, the reality sank in that our work is never finished. Even our time-saving devices seem to only save us time to cram more work-related activities into our lives. Work not finished? Sorry, you can't play.

One wise and honest mother said, "I have a tendency to want to get everything done before I play, which is impossible. So needless to say I am too focused on work and not play. I don't play enough with my girls, but I love the times we do play—the laughter, the craziness, and the connectedness we experience." Her understanding is echoed by many mothers who know it feels great to play, but believe they have way too many things to do before they can.

One mother likened her struggle to that of poor Martha in the Gospels when Jesus came for a visit. The societal expectations of a woman who had houseguests imposed a hefty burden of preparing and serving food and providing comfort. This mother said, "I believe that our society continues to pressure women to be Marthas, and that makes it difficult for so many of us to abandon a messy kitchen for some play. It's taken me a while to figure out that if I strive to meet those Martha standards, I will never feel free to play because the chores will never be done! And in the end, I will be as resentful as the Martha in the Bible story." Writer and mother Jennie Bishop gave me this wonderful essay to share:

> Play is not an easy thing for me. I grew up on a family farm where life was wonderful, but we were taught to always be "productive." My mom's motto was, "There's always something to do if you just open your eyes." As a mother myself, this worked to my advantage when I had a hard or unsavory task to finish, but it also made life difficult because I never felt "finished," and guilt overcame me if I took leisure time to myself. I sometimes felt overwhelmed with my household tasks, homeschool, ministry at our church, and my ministry as an author and speaker. Learning to take time for intimacy with God and my family has been an ongoing challenge.
>
> Fortunately, I serve a loving God who managed to get me married to a rock-and-roll musician who is a kid at heart himself. Randy is in the difficult business of teaching his "serious" wife the great value of play and leisure.
>
> A couple of months ago I lost my mother. Afterward, for obvious reasons, I was not myself. Neither were my daughters.

After a month off because of family events, homeschool was a constant battle.

My approach was to keep going, to push through, to stick to the schedule, and control the day's events. But my husband took me aside. He knew we had been cooped up in the house during an extremely cold winter season, and we needed to get out. I was reluctant to skip a homeschool day because we had already missed so much because of my mother's illness, but I could see that we were about to blow. My nine-year-old and I had ended up in tears the day before.

"Let's go sledding," my wise husband said. We headed to Frankenmuth, a nearby Bavarian tourist village with a giant sledding hill and a café with the finest hot chocolate for miles.

After sledding (or rolling) down the hill enough times to keep our breath from freezing in our noses on a one-degree morning, we trudged across the park to a bridge over a frozen creek that led to an outdoor amphitheater.

"The snow queen lived there," Randy whispered to our six-year-old. "And a troll lives under this bridge to guard the way there."

"There ought to be a troll under that bridge on the way back," I said.

"Why don't you go for it?" said my husband.

So while Randy interpreted the German writing on the walls of the amphitheater to read: "The Snow Queen commands that all who stand in her castle must sing a song," and began to sing "I'm a Little Teapot," I hurried back to the bridge.

"Where's Mom?" I heard Dad shout. "Oh, no, the troll must have gotten her!"

Under the footbridge on the frozen creek, I knew my husband had plotted against me. But it was okay. I understood. It was good for me to play, and he was just making another opportunity for me to loosen up. The girls shrieked with delight when the troll appeared out of nowhere, and we all laughed and headed back up the hill for a few more runs.

Escaping the schedule to play is very important for me to maintain balance. For years I didn't even know that I needed this outlet. But my husband made it clear to me that it was all right to take time out to play with the girls or to have some adult play. Some of the getaways that we as a couple and family have taken have been the best memories of my life. What did John Lennon say... "Life is what happens to you while you're busy making other plans"? My husband has taught me to stop planning unrealistically and start doing more living. I believe this is God's idea, and I'm grateful to have a husband who is encouraging me to learn and practice it.

As I thanked Jennie for sharing this story, I told her I sincerely hope we unleash a whole army of trolls as other mothers read her story.

2. *In this world of comparisons and competition, I don't want to set myself up for another failure.* A second reservation we have about play is that when comparison and competition are on the line, it is quite natural to be afraid we'll mess up or look silly. What if we don't do it "right"? We don't want to be embarrassed or look incompetent. Besides, what if our kids actually beat us at Monopoly? Many of us grew up with activities that celebrated a win/lose mentality. We may have played games like musical chairs or dodgeball when we were little with the focus on the elimination of participants. The whole point of the game was to foster competition and produce losers. We

equate play with those feelings and don't want to reengage or encourage others to participate in losing propositions.

3. *Life is serious. There are just more important things to do in this world than play.* Yet another play aversion stems from what we believe to be important as adults: "Most of us are time-conscious and future-minded—and we want our children to value the same things. We want to see results and are critical of our own mistakes. We may even believe that the benefits of play—imagination, creativity, fun—may lead to bad work habits later on."[2] We have ideas about what we think are important traits, sometimes born out of comparing ourselves to others, and the characteristics displayed in play don't match.

4. *The kids have taken over everything already. I'll just be further consumed if I play rather than be a grown-up.* I can remember looking around my house and not remembering what it looked like before I had children. Their toys were in my former well-appointed family room, their clothes were in my former sewing room, their special cups and utensils were in my once pristine kitchen cabinets, and their sounds were all over my once serene airwaves. I was going to be doggoned if I was going to give up my last shred of adulthood to get on the floor and play. I was sure I would go over the edge into complete child absorption if I didn't keep an arm's length away from their childlike activities, otherwise known as play. That would signal the final blurring of the line between me as the adult and them as the children.

What Is Play?

We learn new things, reawaken activities that we forgot we loved, and see the world through new eyes when we play. Children are so proficient at exploratory play because, ideally, they haven't succumbed to choices, comparisons, and competitions as much as adults have. Their receptors are clear to really see what they look at, to listen to what they hear, to taste what they put in their mouths, and to feel what they touch. They see more sunsets, laugh at more crickets, savor more ice cream, and hear more birds. This truth came to rest in my heart one day as my preschool son and I were getting into our van to go grocery shopping. It was a beautiful spring morning, freshly washed by a predawn shower. A bird was singing in a front yard tree beside our garage. As I closed my van door, Grant said, "Mommy, did you hear that bird singing before we got into the van?" I told him I hadn't heard the bird, but I was so glad he noticed that kind of thing. After a moment's pondering he asked, "Mommy, will I be able to hear the birds sing when I'm a grown-up?" Ouch.

Play is delighting in being alive. When we play, we put aside the demands of life to simply enjoy God's creation, which includes the remarkable people he has put into our lives. That's why the Play Lifesaver is so important. It gives us mini soul vacations whenever we use it. It is a Sabbath in a world of constant striving to get things done, to get ahead, or to make an impression.

The Benefits of Play

We more readily give ourselves permission to experience the Play Lifesaver when we understand and live our Divine Assignments. By understanding our call and the calls of our children, it's easier to grasp that play can be a natural part of our day, our week, our year. We know that play and work each have meaningful and restorative places in our lives. We may even come to realize that without play, we don't work very well.

When we play, we reaffirm our trust in God. We understand that all is in divine order, so when our souls are telling us it's time to rest and relax, we can do so without fearing all of our work will fall apart while we are rejuvenating. We know that God is competent and reliable to handle this remarkable creation and all that is in it without our relentless assistance. We aren't responsible for keeping everything running 24/7. That's God's job.

A common characteristic of all the Lifesavers is that they can help us heal from childhood wounds or recover from holes in the nurture or education we received. Jeanne Zornes found this to be true in her experiences of playing with her children through reading and discovering a love of books:

> My public library helped me survive motherhood, which came during my tired-out late thirties. Once a week the children's librarian put on a "story hour" for preschoolers and mothers. Little did she know that the weary older mother doing finger plays with her little son and daughter was there for personal revival.
>
> My twosome also knew they could push back bedtime if they successfully pleaded "one more chapter" before prayers and lights off. They thought they were making Mom work harder. They had no clue that reading our piles of children's library books was my "play."
>
> I loved those warm, freshly bathed bodies cuddling me under an afghan on the couch while I read.
>
> I missed all that when I was young. My childhood bedtime stories came from a big volume of 365 stories, each one only one page long in big print, quickly read. I never was taken as a child to a library for fun. As a teen and young adult, I viewed libraries as places to do "research," not have a good time.
>
> So when I got married and had children, I decided to change my relationship with libraries. My children and I would *play* at the library. I established a rule of ten books per

child with Mom given censor privileges ("Remember, none about witches"). We staggered out with our armloads, often returning in less than a week for more. I knew if the kids were cranky or having a bad day, I could dangle "go to the library" as a bribe for better behavior.

I had the time of my life learning about bulldozers, bugs, ballet, and beads. I identified with little comic pigs who tried to go on diets but found the carnival food too tempting. I appreciated—probably more than my kids—the big universal questions in some retold folk tales.

Yes, I also read to my children from Bible story and devotional books, to observe the admonition in Deuteronomy 6:7-9 to make teaching about God a part of talking, sitting, walking, lying down and getting up, and even decorating one's home. But many of those books we got from the public library afforded spiritual teaching. If a character had a rotten attitude or made a bad choice, some brief mother-editorializing took place right away.

Today my little ones are in college. Some boxes in their closets hold the "very, very favorite" children's books we bought at school carnivals or that they received as gifts. A few fill a bookshelf just outside their bedrooms where, when they were older, I sat on the floor to read while they got ready for bed.

Don't tell a soul, but a few nights ago I snitched one of those books. It had been a while since I spent time with Brighty, the legendary burro of the Grand Canyon whose escapades made print through Marguerite Henry. I'll finish it another night, but right now I'm "playing" in the Narnia classics.

What I love about Jeanne's description is she "decided to change her relationship with libraries." Even though her childhood had taught her one thing about playing, she decided to learn something new. I love that—and the way she describes the warm, freshly bathed bodies snuggling under the afghan.

A new breed of play emerging in the last decade fosters cooperation over competition. When we experience the pleasure of cooperation rather than the pressure of competition, we might be more inclined to play and to view our world from an abundance mentality rather than a zero sum game. In other words, we would know that there are oceans of love and life in God's creation, and if one person has some of it, that doesn't mean there is less for us. This kind of play encourages people to work together to bring about a greater common good rather than to beat and eliminate the poor souls who are weaker, slower, or not as clever.

The same qualities that play can ignite in children can be very beneficial for mothers. Playing encourages children to develop resourcefulness and originality, and to develop such skills as listening, sharing, and planning. A good dose of play may help moms who feel they have lost some of these qualities to actually learn from children. I know I could benefit from increased skills in listening, sharing, and planning!

Sarah is the mother of two school-aged children. She offers this perspective on the importance of play: "Play is an essential part of my family's life. It helps us to live in the moment and not feel quite so overwhelmed. I believe that through play we strengthen relationships and gain perspective. In my family, we like to say that a good way to learn a lot about someone quickly is to play a board game with them! I think the secret to successful play is focusing on enjoying the other person's company."

One tremendous benefit to play is it can teach us to lighten up. "Children have a remarkable talent for not taking the adult world with the kind of respect we are so confident it ought to be given. To the irritation of authority figures of all sorts, children expend considerable energy in 'clowning around.' They refuse to appreciate the gravity of our monumental concerns, while we forget that if we were to become more like children our concerns might not be so monumental."[3]

Play can teach us that all of our activities and moments are more interconnected than we think. We don't have to view the world in black and white, work against play. Life can be all the colors of the rainbow. Our families can learn to play to get things done. Our routines don't have to be exclusively divided into work or play. What if they are merged into work *and* play? Sing instructions for pouring milk, dance on the way to the bathroom to brush teeth, play "pick up the toys" during a good game of chase. One of my favorite ways to play with my son is a good game of hide and seek. I'm a little sneaky in the way I do this. As I go room to room looking for him, I pick up and put away things. And I usually hide lying or sitting down so I can grab a couple of quiet minutes to myself.

How Do We Get More Play into Our Lives?

The nature of play in your house is going to be unique to your home. There are several factors that affect how your family will choose to play:

 the personality of your children

 your own balance between being at work and spending time with your family

 interests of each family member

 age range of your children

Sarah says her family integrates play into their daily routine as more of an attitude. They laugh at themselves and keep things light while doing daily chores. A significant benefit she reports from this playful spirit is the decrease in sibling bickering as they carry out their tasks. They also love to include their pets as contributors to the playful spirit they seek to nurture. Their pets can lighten serious moments and add silliness as the humans entertain themselves with a game of "What do you think the pet would say to this?"

A group of mothers I talked with came up with a wonderful idea. Figure out what you are going to do anyway, then invite your kids to play with you. Little did they realize how theologically powerful this suggestion is. God knew he was going to create the heavens and the earth and all therein. That was the task he set before himself. But did God do this as drudgery? Absolutely not! God decided to use this task as an opportunity to play. He used wide varieties of color, species, textures, terrain, and sounds to invite his children to play with him. He even said to his first children, "Play with me. Help me name these remarkably goofy creatures that surround you." Invite your children into your space and into your activity. Our children often seem needy because they sense we are inaccessible to them. When you are cooking and cleaning, give them ways to be with you and to be involved while you are laughing, talking, and singing along the way.

Tone of voice is a powerful application of play. Michele says she and her family play in their conversations and in how they verbally handle stressful situations. She relates that a wonderful tension reducer for all of them is to keep the tone light, choosing to prefer banter and humor. They stay connected through play-filled words and a lighthearted tone in the home.

Mothers who are happy and know how to play also report one other understanding that keeps their heads above water: They know they are still in charge and claim the right to establish limits—set timers, lay out ground rules for noise and safety, be firm about the difference between indoor and outdoor activities. Just because you are going to play doesn't mean you completely revert to a childish mind-set.

Does God Play?

God loves to play. If you don't believe that, you haven't spent any time watching puppies, eating chocolate, walking barefoot on the beach, listening to birds sing in the morning, or smelling cookies as they bake. One mindful trip through a day paying attention to your senses—the first five gifts God gave us—is enough to prove to anyone that God loves to play. The very incarnation of God, Jesus Christ, said that the most fundamental nature of the kingdom of God is in the heart of those who are by nature the most playful— children. They are ideally unencumbered by the stresses of choice, comparison, and competition. When we learn from children how to enjoy, explore, and express the wonder of life, we are most aligned with God's intention for his kingdom.

And God's intention for his kingdom and for play is joy. The mind-set and heart-set of this Play Lifesaver is that you cultivate pleasure and fun in living no matter what you are doing. Mothers who practice play know they have a choice—they can either feel cranky about everything they do in a day's time or they can feel joyful and lighthearted. The truth is, if you are sitting on the floor building a truck out of blocks and feeling miserable, you are not practicing play. Yet if you are cooking dinner and joyfully instructing your preteen in making rice, you are a mother at play.

The bottom line is to engage in activities that make you laugh, make you feel free, and help you see the world through the magical, wonder-filled eyes of your children. Learn from your children the art of playing instead of teaching them the imprisonment of stress and perfection. As one wise mother who understood the practice and purpose of play stated about sports, "We're not in this for college scholarships or professional sports. The kids are in this to have fun. At the point they don't have fun, it's not worth it." Let's turn the tide of adult altercations at youth sporting events and counter the desire to push our children to developmental excellence before they hit preschool. Let's learn to play joyfully as women who seek to glorify and enjoy God forever.

Search and Rescue

1. *Warm up*—What was your favorite game growing up? What is your favorite game now?

2. What did you learn about play as you were growing up?

3. Do you find it easy or difficult to play?

4. Respond to this quote by Hugo Rahner: "To play is to yield oneself to a kind of magic." What kind of wonder and fun is missing from your life? What could help you recapture it?

5. Reflect on Jesus' saying the kingdom of God is made up of those with a childlike spirit. What do you think he meant? What connection is there between what he said and the fact that kids are active "play-ers"?

6. How can knowing and living your Divine Assignment help you balance work and play?

7. Ask God to bring to mind a time when he was delighted in your playing. Write out his answer.

8. *Assignment for the upcoming week*—Make a conscious effort once this week to put aside work to play. Note how you feel and what you learn from your reactions.

11

The Touch Lifesaver

*I long to accomplish a great and noble task, but it is
my chief duty to accomplish small tasks as if
they were great and noble.*

—HELEN KELLER

As we walked through the woods, I realized I hadn't had much
time with three-year-old Madison because of my work
schedule and the demands of our household. It was one of those
sacramental moments when the Spirit of God whispered in my ear,
"Reach down and give her a hug." I'm not always very good at
obeying God, but this seemed like a perfectly wonderful suggestion.

As I knelt down to hug Madison, I realized I didn't want to let
go. Madison didn't want to, either. In her sweet, preschool voice she
said, "I love you, Mommy." It was then I resolved to hug often and
to "let them let go first." Whenever my children and I embrace, I let
them make the move to get away from me.

We're Just Big Babies

The Touch Lifesaver has great significance for the healthy development of our children, and it can be a continual source of renewal
and healing for us as mothers. Through touch we communicate

reverence for the body. Through healthy touch we let our children know they are nurtured, protected, and revered. As any mother of an infant knows, our bodies are remarkably fragile. It takes all of us working together to care for each of us throughout our lives. By our touch, children know they are cared for, and their bodies are remarkable creations to be honored and maintained.

Through touch we connect with others in a way that transcends words. My friend Susan shared this powerful and very beautiful story of a corner she turned after her second child was born.

> After Caroline was born, I had a hard time bonding with her. I did not seem to have the instant "love" for her that came when I had Christopher. I was in a bad place. I was angry, depressed, and overwhelmed by all the medical problems. I began therapy to help me see her as my daughter, as a child of God, instead of just a baby who had all these mental and physical challenges. During one session, the therapist asked, "Do you ever hold Caroline just for the sake of holding her?" I answered, "No." He recommended I do this, and then let him know if it helped.
>
> I did exactly that. I held Caroline, just held her close to me, wrapping my arms all around her. It was the first time I actually felt close to her emotionally and felt love for her as my child. And because of that, I wanted to hold her as much as possible. Holding her helped me relax and let go of all the negative feelings I had inside. I know that it helped her, too.

We heal, share empathy, and comfort through touch. Karen says her daughter, who is now a teenager, still looks for the comfort of her mom when she scrapes a knee, cuts her finger, or bumps her head. Simply holding someone enables them to relax deeply and release restricted feelings of stress and anxiety. Lovingly caressing those we love gives them a renewed sense of positive body image and healthy self-esteem. We give them an awareness of acceptance and feeling integrated into the community. "Touch transcends language and personality. It speaks directly to the innermost core of the human heart, soothing away pain and dissolving tension from body and mind."[1]

While touch is initially thought of as simply physical, it also has educational, emotional, and mental ramifications. Studies show that children who are sitting next to someone they love learn to read more quickly than those who do not have this connection. The physical closeness and reassurance of touch lets them know it is not dangerous to try the words, make mistakes, and learn.

Babies who are abandoned in the hospital at birth and don't receive cuddling and physical nurture beyond basic-needs care show "failure to thrive." They become listless and disinterested in eating and socialization. And the truth is, the need to be touched in a caring way does not stop with the onset of adulthood. We're all grown-up babies in this respect. Adults as well as babies have what one mother describes as "skin need," or the yearning for the soothing reassurance of being touched.

Donnae, whose five boys are now all grown and out of her nest, illustrates this point: "We have always been a huggy, touchy kind of group. When my kids were small, they loved to sit on my lap, have me touch their heads and rub their backs. My youngest especially loved to have his head rubbed as he went to sleep. Now that he is grown, it's funny, but he still loves to have his head rubbed, especially when he is stressed."

Don't Touch Me!

What about kids who don't like physical touch? Maybe your child is incredibly active and doesn't want to spend much time cuddling. As our kids become teenagers they may become more cautious about hugging, kissing, holding hands, and walking arm in arm. Sometimes we have an older, adopted child who came to us with a history that makes physical contact unpleasant. Some autistic children shy away from physical connection. How do we maintain the emotional and spiritual bond that physical touch affords?

What if a mother finds touch uncomfortable? Through upbringing or inborn preference, she may find she's not as prone to physical contact as others around her. As one mother described, "I wasn't physical with my son. I had my own childhood issues to deal with before I could open myself up that way." Mothers may have their own history of touch deficiency or touch abuse. Does this mean these moms are headed for unhappiness?

The way we live out the Touch Lifesaver is going to be configured and lived out as individually as the people who practice it. Each mother is going to feel well suited to some of the Lifesavers and not as drawn to others. You and your child may simply have different styles. Your daughter may be a cactus, and you're a cocker spaniel. Your son may be a stuffed teddy bear, while you're a real bear. Whatever the combination, the trick is to realize that touch is a matter of preference and not expectation.

A devoted mother says, "I'm not physical by nature. But I try to faithfully hug my children before bed, look into their eyes, and tell them I love them, that Jesus loves them, and that I am glad God gave them to me. I hold their hands a lot...and not just to keep them from running into the street."

If you find you prefer less physical touch, it may be helpful and healing to determine why you feel that way. You may discover that touch was unpleasant or dangerous for you as a child. If this is the case, guidance from a respected advisor regarding those childhood wounds could lead you to realize that the touch of those who love you in your current environment is a healer of memories and perspectives that are keeping you from initiating or responding to touch. Lifesavers can heal and restore us to a fullness of life as they are lived out in love and respect.

One of my friends who is not physical by nature highlights a potent perspective. We can touch our children through all of their senses. She seeks to touch her children through the look in her eyes and the tone and words she uses when she speaks to them. If a child doesn't want to be physically touched or if a mom doesn't prefer physical touch, ask, "How can we touch without using our skin receptors?"

Touch with the Other Senses

When you seek to touch your children through their sense of sight, you may use facial expressions such as a smile or a wink. The nonverbal cues you give your children are powerful in helping them feel either safe or unwanted. Many times they will pick up a nonverbal cue over what you actually say.

Little love notes and emails are other influential ways to touch your children when they don't want to be hugged. Get in the practice of writing a note on her mirror, taping a particularly good quote to his computer monitor, leaving loving scripture on her pillow, including a surprise message in his backpack or lunch bag. Touching children in this way is nonthreatening for them since they don't have to respond right away, yet they know you have thought about them and care enough to communicate love.

The sense of hearing also brings opportunities for "touch." Without prompting, put her favorite CD into the player as you get into the van to run errands. Sing a song that is special to him. Give compliments, encouragement, and affection through your words. Let your children overhear you talking positively about them.

Children seem to love to talk at bedtime. Whether it's a diversionary tactic or not, let them have a few minutes to debrief at the end of the day. These chats can have an amzing influence on the bond you have with your children, no matter how old they are.

One compelling way to touch others using the sense of hearing is to apologize. Unresolved conflicts and untended wounds may in fact be the reason there is a block in physical touch. Apologizing for a mistake builds love, regard, and trust. It clears the air. Talking through a blunder can give your child increased comfort in knowing that even Mommy is not perfect. Apologies and forgiveness forge durable bonds as individuals are truly touched by the intimacy of the exchange.

As a baking commercial once stated, "Nothing says lovin' like something from the oven." Whether you are a wonderful cook or not, you can touch your kids in an intoxicating way by filling the air they breathe with the smell of something they love to eat. Even if you purchase premade cookie dough, frozen lasagna, or refrigerated bread dough, the effort you make in putting pleasing smells into your home is always rewarded. Our most powerful memory evoker is our sense of smell. You touch your family with love and good memories when you offer them scents that bring them comfort and anticipation.

Similarly, if your kids are too old for a hug when they are feeling blue, they never seem to outgrow the comfort of a chocolate chip cookie. Keep a list of the foods your children respond to positively. Remind them often of your affection and care for them by having those foods in their lives. My children are often surprised and delighted when they open the cupboard to find a snack that I bought at the store. When they say, "Mom, I love this!" I respond, "I know. I was at the store today thinking about how much I love you. I bought that just for you." They eat the snack with a smile, having been touched by Mommy's love and knowing Mommy thought of them during the day.

Never underestimate the power of the touch you have on your children when they know they have touched you. One Sunday morning that also happened to be Nancy's birthday, her daughter Rebecca told her there was a surprise at church. Nancy had no idea what it could be. The revelation came in "Big Church" during the service when Rebecca's choir performed "Joyful, Joyful, We Adore Thee," Nancy's favorite hymn. Nancy said, "Through my tears there was her little face just beaming." Reciprocal touch has dynamic bonding capability.

A Touch of Affirmation

Practicing touch is affirming life. When you lovingly attend to the physical part of a person, you let him know that his body is important and should be treated as the remarkable instrument of God it was created to be. The apostle Paul speaks of our bodies in his first letter to the Corinthians as "a sacred place, the place of the Holy Spirit" (6:19 THE MESSAGE). By touch, you affirm that all of life is sacred, including our physical life so lovingly provided for by our highly ingenious Creator. By staying in touch with your physical surroundings through all of your senses, you root yourself in the "stuff" God has made. That connection promotes balance, perspective, and healthy choices. That connection helps you sail in comfort and peace on the S.S. Sanity.

Search and Rescue

1. *Warm up*—What is your favorite fabric? Why?

2. Describe a time when you enjoyed the touch of your children.

3. Why do you think God created us with "skin need"?

4. Are you comfortable where you are on the touch spectrum or would you like to change one way or the other? Is your family more or less inclined to be physically affectionate?

5. Make a chart for each of your family members. Include in this chart what you think their favorites are in the areas of sight, sound, touch, scent, and taste. Make it part of a family discussion to check out your predictions, and then post the amended chart for the entire family to see.

6. How can you stay "in touch" with a child who doesn't prefer physical touch by nature or by developmental phase?

7. Why do we affirm life when we affirm our physical needs? What does it mean to you that our bodies are the home of the Holy Spirit? What does that say to you about your children and their physical selves?

8. In a love letter to God, thank him for each of your senses. Tell him what you most enjoy about each of these five gifts.

9. *Assignment for the upcoming week*—While hugging your kids, practice "let them let go first." How do you respond? How do they respond?

12

The Recording Lifesaver

Remember me with favor, O my God.

—NEHEMIAH 13:31

"Scattered." That one word is what many mothers use to describe themselves when they are overboard. Synonyms are strewn, dispersed, diffused, spread out. It is usually something that is done *by* someone *to* something. Most of the time, moms don't want to be scattered. We don't like feeling controlled by the schedule and the commitments. We don't want to feel as if we're leaving ourselves in a hundred little pieces all over the place. Our hearts are scattered, our brains are scattered, our emotions are scattered, and you may as well forget what has happened to our identity and intentions!

In the book of Nehemiah, "scattered" is a key word used in the story of the Jewish people. The nation has been scattered because the people ignored their identity and their Divine Assignment among other nations. Nehemiah is grieved because they are aimless and seem to be forgotten. In the first chapter of his story, Nehemiah laments to God as he reflects on the state of his people, his family:

> Remember the instruction you gave to your servant Moses, saying, "If you are unfaithful, I will scatter you among the nations, but if you return to me and obey my commands,

then even if your exiled people are at the farthest horizon, I will gather them from there and bring them to the place I have chosen as a dwelling for my Name" (1:8-9).

Three times in the last chapter of Nehemiah, the prophet pleads with God, "Remember me." He wants to be remembered for the good things he did for God and in the service of God. He wants to be remembered with mercy by God. Nehemiah is, in essence, asking God to cherish and validate the connection they have. Nehemiah ends the entire book with this one sentence, a heartfelt request, "Remember me with favor, O my God."

This appeal comes in a book that is full of a "cupbearer overboard." Nehemiah receives word that his family is in shambles. Their identity is muddled, their territory is ruined, and their sense of dignity in the region is squashed. They have intermingled with those outside the faith for so long they have no idea who they are anymore. Further, they are ridiculed and trampled by those around them because they are perceived to be weak and ineffective. They don't understand their original Divine Assignment, and they have completely lost a vision for their uniqueness.

Nehemiah's greatest asset is his unwavering belief that he and his family are unique and need to maintain their uniqueness. Without it, they will be ineffective in their world. They will be weak and pitiful; they will be at the mercy of the forces around them.

Nehemiah's strategy? Help the family members remember who they are and build a strong symbol of their identity. Nehemiah understands that the word "remember" literally means "put back together that which is dismembered," to re-member. He brings the pieces of his family together, uniting them with a task and ultimately an identity. He not only rallies the nation of Israel to rebuild the walls of Jerusalem, he imports the priest Ezra to remind the people of the words that have been important to their distinctiveness for centuries. He gives them tangible and identifiable symbols of their uniqueness (and of God's powerful presence in their history), then brings out the scrapbooks, if you will, of all their family has been through, where they have had moments of faithfulness, and where they still need to learn and draw closer to God.

Nehemiah restores, records, and remembers. The result is a powerful sense of identity, a renewed centeredness for his family, and increased effectiveness to carry out God's Divine Assignment for the nation. The nation is re-gathered and re-membered.

Nehemiah proves to be a man of both prayer and action. Read his story in the Old Testament. Use a good study Bible to get the full impact of the narrative. Nehemiah is a wonderful role model for a mom trying to establish strength, identity, and impact for her family.

No one wants to be forgotten. The inscription of the yearbook says, "Remember me." A young parent who is dying says to the other, "Please don't let the kids forget me." Family members living far apart send cards and emails to remind the others, "I'm still here. Don't forget me in the rush of your everyday life." To be forgotten is equated with being insignificant, to have lived a life that is not meaningful or memorable to others. We want to be remembered because we don't want to be forgotten.

We all want to be thought of for our contributions and to authenticate our identity. In the end, what we want to know is "I matter!" As a mother, you will not only "save" your own life, but the lives of your family members when you use the Recording Lifesaver, when you act as the family journalist.

The Family Journalist

The backbone of journalistic writing, one of the most potent recording systems we have in our society, is seeking answers to the questions Who? What? When? Where? and Why? Most of our news-paper and magazine reading centers around these goals:

 Entertainment—We want to find laughter in the comics, enlightenment through the arts, and titillation through gossip pages.

 Information—We seek "how to" instruction on a variety of topics from home improvement to relationship enhancement.

 Integration of the things happening around us—As we look at the different sections of the paper, we discover how the stock market is affecting global trade, how the weather patterns are influencing commerce in various parts of the world, and how political decisions affect our local, regional, national, and global communities.

 Looking into the mirror of society to see how we fit in—We ingest the lives of others and gauge our own lives by what we find. We see the opportunities available and note what other people are doing, then ask ourselves, "Where do I fit in?"

Sometimes the news is earth-shaking. I will never forget the morning as a teenager delivering the daily *Washington Post* when the biggest headline I ever witnessed said "Nixon Resigns." Sometimes the news is tucked into a diminutive corner where no one but the affected family even bothers to look. In either case, and all those in between, recording history for humor, bonding, and perspective gives us a dynamic sense of where we have been and where we might be going.

The Recording Lifesaver has many of the same functions. We are looking for ways to entertain, inform, integrate, and understand our place in the world. Moms on the S.S. Sanity find ways to act as reporters and interpreters as their families develop.

Who?

The moms who are happiest in this Lifesaver don't go it alone. They encourage the whole family to get into the act. Let your kids and husband write down their own thoughts on family events and activities. Not only does this ease mom's burden of managing and arranging everything by herself, it brings to light what others think is important. When we get our children involved with the practice, we gain powerful clues to their "unfolding" (talked about in Chapter 6). While we're focused on what we think has meaning, it's critical to note what the children think is worth noting. We find out what they think is funny and instructional. This can be indicative of their personalities. Given four cameras on the same trip, we're likely to get four different sets of prints.

What?

Most obviously we record the milestones and celebrations. In life's symphony, this is the melody or the tune that is most apparent. Obvious high points can provide recurring themes such as vacations, birthdays, and occasions that mark the developmental phases of life. Donnae notes a gift she gave to one of her sons: "Photos have become increasingly important. I made an album for my oldest son and his wife showing their baby pictures, photographs of when they were two-, five-, and nine-year-olds, teen pictures (when they met), wedding pictures, then photos of their babies. I gave it to my daughter-in-law for Mother's Day last year. They still have it on their coffee table." This gift provided the strong melody of positive comparisons in milestone pictures, the celebration of marriage, and the wonder of a new generation forming. Supporting the momentous, Donnae also used the everyday events like a symphony also employs undertones. These harmony notes aren't always obvious, yet they provide the background support for the memorable melody. Our lives are more lived at home than on vacation. The power of recording for the present and the future lies in capturing the essence of the everyday. That's where we live; that's where we are ultimately formed.

Nancy notes, "I have a family history for both me and my husband that I will share with the girls when they are older." While it is not necessarily visually entertaining or resplendent in detail, the written documents of family history provide the backdrop for understanding nuances and the formation of character and belief in those who came before us. Don't neglect the commonplace.

Linda offered this:

> I love to make books with my kids. We've done all types—the usual picture albums and scrapbooks. However, we've also done some unusual things. My daughter has a biblical name (Sarah), so we did a little book on the background of her name. My children want to get baptized in April. We're putting together a book about it—why they want to do this and their feelings.
>
> This is a Lifesaver to me because when you record important (or quaint) events as they happen, you can later go back and read about them and be encouraged. We have what we call a "comfort box" at our house. One of the items in the box is a book in which I've written funny, clever, or heartwarming stories about the kids. Whenever someone is feeling "down," we go get the "comfort box" and read one of the stories. It always lifts our spirits.

Now, just the other day, my delightful son, Grant, brought me a treasure he requested be placed in his scrapbook. It was a dinosaur bandage he had just peeled off his elbow. He said, "It's the best Band-Aid I've ever had, Mom. I would really like to keep it." It's still sitting on my dresser as I write, waiting for me to decide what I'll ultimately do with this piece of history.

When?

Libby's family makes good use of everyday time to collect, record, and remember. "We specifically do a lot of storytelling, a lot of oral history. Almost every dinnertime we have 'remember when' discussions, and bedtime is prime time for short stories from when Scott and I were kids."

Nancy's family has a unique way to record and recall significant events. They have a jar in which they put slips of paper that have memorable or noteworthy events written on them as they occur throughout the year, such as "first babysitting job" or "horseback riding during spring break." On New Year's Eve or Day, they pull out each one and remember the year that has just passed.

Where?

As moms, we will each have our own mode of recording and specific places where we will keep those memories. Some of us love technology, so our recording is kept on video- and audiotapes or CDs. Some of us love crafting, and our memories are kept in scrapbooks or handcrafted items such as quilts and watercolor pictures. Some of us love collecting. We find our method of recording is a compilation of old family recipes or all of the stuffed animals anyone in our family past and present ever had. "We take pictures and keep special cards, tickets, and keepsakes. We each have a drawer in our bedrooms where 'specials' are kept, even though we didn't plan it that way. It kind of developed over time," notes Libby.

Some of us love writing so we keep journals, calendars, and letters. Lynn offers these avenues for recording: "I keep a 'Mother's Journal' on the computer. I write regular family letters at Christmas and keep a copy in a notebook. My husband and I both have acquired a 'Legacy' book that we are filling out with memories of our own childhoods and hope that someday they will be valued by our children and grandchildren." We might even have a simple spiral notebook we keep in the diaper bag for little notes as we can fit them into our day. If there is an older sibling in the house, have them write down the funny things that are said. Original, preserved handwriting can provide some of the most precious souvenirs we have.

Find whatever means fits best with your talents, interests, and time constraints. You may find this changes through the years. The important thing is simply to do it.

Why?—The Heart of the Lifesaver

The importance of the everyday is highlighted in this observation by Frederick Buechner:

> A sacrament is when something holy happens. It is transparent time, time which you can see through to something deep inside time.
>
> Needless to say, church isn't the only place where the holy happens. Sacramental moments can occur at any moment, at any place, and to anybody. Watching something get born. A walk on the beach. Somebody coming to see you when you're sick. A meal with people you love. Looking into a stranger's eyes and finding out he's not a stranger.

If we weren't blind as bats, we might see that life itself is sacramental.[1]

When I asked Patti how she and her family record she said,

I love to take photos of all the activities and special occasions of our lives, in particular, vacations. Every time I take the film to be developed, I can't wait to get it back and once I do, I get so excited thinking how I can use the pictures in my scrapbooks! I am a firm believer that every family has a story to tell, and I am trying to take good pictures and put good journal entries and descriptions within each scrapbook. I want my kids to have our family history documented through written communication and photos. I don't want our family photos and history to fall to the same fate that my grandmother's has. Still living at the age of 100 years old, she has such wonderful photos and heritage to share. However, through the years the names of those in the pictures did not get recorded on the backside. Now my grandmother is losing her eyesight and can't see to tell us who is in the pictures.

As a family, we all love to go back and look through the finished pages of a scrapbook and reflect on the precious memories we've built through the years. We value our scrapbooks so much that as part of our family fire escape plan, we would run to grab the scrapbooks first (well, of course, after the kids!). In addition to the scrapbooks, we record lots of memories on our video camera. Often on Friday nights we will pull out the old home videos and watch them together as a family—what fun for all of us!

Patti's response highlights three primary reasons to record. First, we record because it brings us joy. True joy is found by living firmly in the present. The Recording Lifesaver helps keep us in the present. Constantly look at life through the lens of: "Would this be a great picture?" "That was a really remarkable insight Junior just had," and "I want to affirm that character trait I just saw Sweet Pea exhibit." Recording helps us shed ruminations of yesterday, worries of tomorrow, and the comparisons of the present. When we are so focused on our own families such that we are vigilant for the recordable moment, we don't really have time to be concerned with anyone else's business or worried that they're concerned with ours. We are free. It makes us slow down and think about what's really happening. It keeps us anchored in the present as we are attentive, poised to record in whatever way we find most authentic and convenient.

Second, conscientious recording makes it easier to recall family history. We can honor what has come before us. We can celebrate the lives of those we have never met, yet who have influenced us in the present. When we make it a practice to record our family's life together, we are affirming that each life and the collective life is important. What we choose to record and bring out in the future gives our children vital information regarding what we as parents believe to be important. The pictures they see in the family albums, the stories shared around the table, the home movies, all give them clues about family values and their own uniqueness in that context.

Recording prepares the way for our children to watch their own unfolding. Children love the sense of who they are that comes from retelling stories. They love to hear stories of when you were a child. "When I was your age..." can be the start of some entertaining and enlightening dinner or bedtime conversations. Sharing family stories helps a child develop a sense of her place in family history.

In collecting, recording, and remembering, we give our children touchstones of past successes. We also give them beacons that call them into the future. The more information they have about themselves, especially information they have provided through their spoken and written words, the more richly they can piece together the fabric of their lives.

Third, recording and remembering reinforces family values. We know that behavior that is reinforced is likely to be repeated. What pictures do we take of our kids and in what activities? Those pictures will tell them, "We thought this was noteworthy." "We liked it when you looked like this." "We enjoyed this time with you." The items that we choose to be souvenirs of various events and trips provide clues to them of what we treasure. Why do we love to look at movies of vacations and significant family events? We like to watch the interactions of others, and we gain insight about ourselves from the way other people responded to us.

Transition Management

In addition to these three influential reasons to record, there is a fourth. Recording gives us tools to help us cope with and move through the inevitable transitions of life. And there are always transitions in life. They are commonly the result of crisis, choice, and change.

Crisis. Hopefully, there won't be many truly crisis transitions in our lives. These are the catastrophic shifts that occur through accident or other external, often uncontrollable, events that brings alterations in role and circumstance. They can include illness, layoffs, and unexpected deaths.

Choice. Most transitions in our lives are the result of choice or normal developmental change. Changes in marital status are often based on choice, although it can be a crisis if the choice is not ours. Moving to a new city or job, having a family, going to graduate school, and leaving or reentering the employment world are often choice-based transitions.

Change. Predictable developmental changes include children growing and going to school, moving in and out of holiday periods, interests, and friendship shifting over time, parents aging, and non-catastrophic deaths.

Transition is a natural part of life. The Recording Lifesaver can ease many transitions as we are confident we will be able to remember and recall the times, stages, events, and people who have brought us joy. These elements have, in fact, shaped us and our families into who we are and who we are becoming.

Recording gives us a sense of self. Often in my coaching practice with mothers, I ask them to identify the passions, talents, interests, skills, and character traits that distinguish them or that they enjoy. About 30 percent of the time, this is an agonizing exercise. They look at me with puzzled and anguished eyes and say, "I haven't the slightest idea." It's sad and frightening for them to realize they have lost the zesty uniqueness that makes them a distinct creation of God. My prescription for them is to recollect the best and most robust memories they have of being a child. This will give them clues to the essence of the self-concept that is dormant and buried. If someone did some form of recording for them as children, this task is easier.

Sailing moms know that memories give us tools to teach grace and choice. Some memories may bring a sense of shame or failure. To those memories we apply the reality of God's grace, which gives us a fresh start every day. Some memories may remind us that someone treated us unkindly or unfairly. To those memories we give healing grace to ourselves and eventual forgiveness to others as we are bathed in the knowledge that God loves us dearly.

Some memories give us clarity to say a hearty "yes" to continuing in a pattern that we intentionally choose for our lives as we grow and make further decisions. For example, in looking through a scrapbook, we may realize that there are a lot of pictures of us being involved in helpful projects or having fun planning and putting on events. We may not realize how much we really loved this sort of activity, but seeing that it has been such a big part of our lives and enjoying it so much may give us clues to our identity and further Divine Assignments. We can see what we have loved about our past and choose to have more of it in our present and future.

The beauty of the Recording Lifesaver is that you find yourself aware of what you value and believe to be worth saving.

Why do we record? So we can remember pictures, literally and soulfully, and articulate them as beautifully as Frederick Buechner did when he spoke of this moment with his children:

> I pick the children up at the bottom of the mountain where the orange bus lets them off in the wind. They run for the car like leaves blowing. Not for keeps, to be sure, but at least for the time being, the world has given them back again, and whatever the world chooses to do later on, it can never so much as lay a hand on the having-beeness of this time. In the vast and empty reaches of the universe it can never be otherwise than that when the orange bus stopped with its red lights blinking, these two children were on it. Their noses were running. One of them dropped a sweater. I drove them home.[2]

We record because we know that nothing is for keeps. We record because we don't want our identity and memories to be scattered to the enemies of too fast, too much, too little time for what's really important. We record because we want to share the essence of "having-beeness" with those we love and with those who will come into our future and want to know why we are the way we are. We record to remember the sacramental poignancy of blinking red bus lights, running noses, and dropped sweaters.

Search and Rescue

1. *Warm up*—Are you feeling scattered or gathered?

2. As you look at Nehemiah's story, how does your family seem in relation to the nation of Israel? Are you scattered with a diffused identity and little directions? Or are you feeling strong in family members knowing who they are, why they are here, and how they are significant?

3. How do you keep your family's identity intact? Are there projects you work on together that give you a sense of unity? Are there pieces of family history you review to help everyone remember who and whose they are?

4. How do you like to keep records? Do you do it through writing, picture taking, storytelling, keepsakes, or memorabilia? Knowing that you are very active and there may be little time for this, how would you like to make the most of the time you do have to keep the family's identity in your memories?

5. What are some of the things from your own childhood that you have that help you remember and cherish your past? Respond to this quote by Gabrielle Michonne: "Remember who you *are* by remembering who you *were*."

6. Ask God to show you some significant events and memories that you might want to share with your family. Ask him to show you the best way to recall and retell those memories. Write out his answer.

7. *Assignment for the upcoming week*—Keep a small notebook with you at all times to jot down little things you want to remember, whether you think they'll be significant to anyone else or not.

13

The Healthy Connections Lifesaver

*The most important thing in life is to learn how to give
out love, and to let it come in.*

—MORRIE SCHWARTZ

Indiana Jones is on a quest. His never satiated thirst for adventurous archeological finds has led him to search for the Holy Grail, or the cup believed to be the one Jesus drank from at the Last Supper. Jones' purpose takes him through several countries, harrowing adventures, and a rekindling of his relationship with his father. In the final scene of *Indiana Jones and the Last Crusade* (Paramount, 1989), Indiana enters a sequestered cave in an ancient temple inhabited by a mythical knight who has been waiting 700 years for visitors.

The cave is filled with an array of cups. Indiana must choose the correct one to sample water from a central cistern. He must make this choice quickly as the water in the correct cup will save his father, who is dying from a bullet wound in the temple antechamber. Choosing the wrong cup will be fatal to both of them.

Unknowingly, Indiana has led his enemies to the cave, as well. As he is perusing the choices, they enter and demand to know which is the grail. The knight tells them, "You must choose. But choose wisely. For as the true grail will bring you life, the false grail will take it from you." They rashly pick a highly embellished golden cup. Scooping water from the cistern, the adversary believes he has discovered the secret to eternal life. Instead he disintegrates. The knight shakes his head and wryly affirms the obvious, "He has chosen poorly."

Indiana quickly but carefully chooses a cup he believes to be in keeping with Christ's character, samples the water, and lives. The knight nods approvingly, "You have chosen wisely."

The Healthy Connections Lifesaver is all about choosing wisely.

The Need for Community

When I talk about community, I don't just mean in a civic sense, like your municipal community or your city limits. I mean the people you choose to surround yourself with, as in your church community, your neighborhood community, your friend community, and your family community. I define community as the people you support and the people who support you. Your community may be centered in where you live or in the things that interest you. It may be small or large. Community at its best brings a feeling of belonging and connection.

Mothers often feel isolated. Working in the silos of our families, separated from others by the barriers of comparison and competition, overwhelmed by simply keeping up with the choices we face, we sometimes find it difficult to establish meaningful relationships and nurture a sense of contribution to the community.

We know we don't want to be alone, but we also don't always want to get overly involved either. We may have seen others who are keeping a frantic pace to get everything done on the to-do list. We have heard others say "I'm so busy," and we have understood that is not a badge of honor. We have had conversations with mothers who profess to have no notion of who they are or what they were before they became household mavens. Yet the longing for connection remains.

Two Enemies of Community, One Enemy of Sanity

Sometimes we shy away from community because of *inadequacy*. What do we have to offer, after all? Our house isn't big or nice enough to entertain. We don't seem to possess the skills we see evidenced in people around us who are making a difference. We've been thinking in "child speak" so long we're afraid to talk and reveal we don't have much else going on in our heads. Time, money, and energy are in short supply. We don't have enough to get involved; we aren't enough to get involved.

Self-sufficiency is a second enemy of community. Whether through upbringing, geographic positioning, or a defense mechanism designed to hide our perceived inadequacies, we choose to not need anyone. We can do it ourselves. Our culture lauds the self-made, the independent, the self-regulated.

On the other hand, an enemy to sanity is to be *overly involved*. Some mothers try to escape being overwhelmed with anxiety by volunteering or doing too much in the external community. At times, many feel caught between a rock and a hard place—not wanting to be stuck at home, but not wanting to have life get out of control with too many community demands. With our dignity hanging by a thread, we get wedged in that strange place of always feeling we should be doing one thing when we're doing another. At home keeping the household running? We think we should be at the school volunteering. At school volunteering? We keep thinking of all the things that need to be done at home. We seem to be living two lives, one in the present physical moment and one in the out-of-body experience called "should be doing."

Healthy connection to the community stems from a healthy understanding and implementation of Divine Assignments. The self-esteem and self-control that come from knowing that God has designed us specifically to be in the world at this time and in this place can quench the nagging doubts that we are not doing enough, that we are not really necessary, or that we are supposed to go it alone. With a confident knowledge of our place in this world, we say yes to involvements that reflect and promote our purpose and say no to opportunities that are not supportive or illustrative of our purpose.

Personal style and preferences influence our ability to choose wisely where and how to be involved with others in ways that bring out our natural radiance and dedication. By understanding personality temperament, we get a handle on why some situations and people seem more compatible to us and some seem to bring out the worst in us.

Personality Type and Healthy Connections

The Myers-Briggs Type Indicator (MBTI®) is the most widely used personality typing test in the world. Millions of people have taken various forms of this test. And even if you haven't, you're probably familiar with the four major categories: Introvert/Extrovert, Sensing/Intuitive, Thinking/Feeling, Judgment/Perception. Using the MBTI® in combination with a keen understanding of your Divine Assignment gives you a remarkable set of lenses through which to make good and fitting decisions on how you want to be involved with your community. The goal of this practice is to foster connection and support your God-given desire to make a difference. It hinges on the critical understanding of your temperament and preferences as a unique individual. Your purpose is never the same as those of the people around you. If that were the case, you or your peer would be expendable, since you would be duplicates. The trick to satisfying and meaningful connection is to understand our "specific context" and to embrace that we "count in ways no one else does."

Using the four categories in the Myers-Briggs, let's explore some of your potential preferences for carrying out your purpose in your specific context as no one else can. (If you would like to take the Myers-Briggs, contact me through the information at the back of this book, and I can arrange it with you. There is a charge for this service.)

Do you gain energy from being in a group of people? If so, you are probably an extrovert on the Introvert–Extrovert Scale. If you find you are more energized when you have had time for personal reflection, you are more introverted. This scale measures energy—where you spend it and where you gain it. As an extrovert, you may believe you "should" be spending a certain amount of time each day in quiet meditation, but it actually makes you antsy and cranky. You enjoy the stimulation you find in others. As an introvert, you may think you "ought to" be out in the community or spending lots of time interacting with your kids. However, you may find this actually takes life from you. Where do you get your energy, from being with others or from being alone?

The next category is Sensing–Intuitive. If you process information from the outside in, or are more oriented to your senses, you have a Sensing preference. However, you may find you process information from the inside out, or are more oriented to your intuition. You have an Intuitive preference. Sensing preference mothers like to handle the everyday details of events and the concrete issues of practicality. Intuitive preference mothers are more comfortable leaving the details to others while they focus on the big picture or abstract world of ideas. Trying to force yourself or others to be the opposite of a preference fosters misunderstandings and missed opportunities to partner in projects. Sensing mothers effectively carry out the details of the well-conceived ideas of the Intuitive mothers. Where do you focus? On the details or on the big picture?

Everyone thinks and feels. In the Thinking–Feeling category, one tends to dominate. Some mothers pay more attention to their thoughts, governing with their heads. These women have a Thinking preference. Others give more credence to their feelings and follow their hearts. These mothers have a Feeling preference. Sometimes distinguished as tough-minded and tender-hearted, these two preferences can become polarized and unable to understand each other. Each mother needs to embrace and be comfortable with her style, while appreciating the contribution the other style has to offer. Similarly, mothers who are happy recognize the differences in their own family members and call on those differences to round out discussions and decisions. From where do you make your decisions? Your head or your heart?

A final preference continuum highlights the difference between those who like deadlines and those who do not. Mothers with a Judgment preference make and keep schedules in their daily lives. Mothers with a Perception preference like to keep their options open and do not like being tied to an agenda. Another way to look at this difference is to consider how you shop for an item. Do you like to look at all the alternatives, visit several stores (or entire malls), compare prices, and still stew over the purchase once it has been made? Or do you generally know what you want, walk into a store, purchase it, and think nothing more of it while you go on to the next item on your agenda? If you operate the first way, you have a Perception preference. If you function the second way, you have a Judgment preference.

How do you like your life to flow? From an agenda or from open-ended options?

The bottom line is we are what and who we are as a gift from God. Make wise decisions about where you fit in, who you connect with and how, and how you express yourself and allow others to express themselves. Confident moms use personality information to make decisions about the kind of people and situations they find most nourishing and growth producing. Swimming moms maintain healthy connections that give them opportunities to be authentic and engaged in the way that makes the most sense for them and the greatest positive impact on those around them. And healthy women remember that we need all of us to make the world go round, even if we aren't naturally drawn to some types of people.

So with whom do we need to maintain healthy connections?

In the Beginning

Start with the beginning. The first relationship you ever had, even before you knew you were having it, was with God. That's because God initiated life. God initiated you: "For you created my inmost being; you knit me together in my mother's womb" (Psalm 139:13). And God continues to initiate your life with every breath you take and every thought you think:

> You know when I sit and when I rise; you perceive my thoughts from afar. You discern my going out and my lying down; you are familiar with all my ways. Before a word is on my tongue you know it completely, O LORD. You hem me in—behind and before; you have laid your hand upon me. Such knowledge is too wonderful for me, too lofty for me to attain (Psalm 139:2-6).

Indeed such an understanding of God's deeply intimate relationship with us is too much for us to comprehend. Sometimes that is intimidating as we see how seemingly easy it is for others to relate to God. We long to be aligned with God in a meaningful, relational way.

In their book *Come as You Are*, Betty Southard and Marita Littauer report,

> There is a lot of frustration and many misconceptions about how to [connect with God]. And yes, personalities do experience God in different ways. We found that those who understood why their reactions were different from others—and had come to accept themselves as God created them—were far more likely to have found a meaningful way to connect with God, a way that worked for them. A way that may not correspond to the "myths" they formerly believed.[1]

Indeed, understanding and embracing your preferences and temperament are critical to making healthy and meaningful bonds with the one who made you that way in the first place.

You are unique. You are distinct. You can't judge your relationship with God based on what others find meaningful. You may find you understand God's love for you more in the context of being with others than when you are alone. While some moms find God's presence in nature, others find God speaks to them through the remarkable logic of a mathematical equation. A regularly scheduled time for quiet may hold just what you need to keep your link to God strong. On the other hand, the thought of a regularly scheduled time of solitude may send you screaming off into the sunset. Some mothers find they are on a seemingly endless quest for God, while others are very content to know what they know and don't feel compelled to be on a constant expedition.

Just as God is multifaceted beyond our comprehension, we need each and all of us to help represent God in the world. For example, I have a Divine Assignment of Wholeness, while my friend Claudia has a Divine Assignment of Compassion and my friend Beth has a Divine Assignment of Hospitality. Between us, we make a nice combination for people to understand God's ever-present concern and kindness as we join our Divine Assignments in planning an event or purpose opportunity. You might have a Divine Assignment of Justice, while a neighbor has the Divine Assignment of Mercy. Between you, you form a larger understanding of the nature of God than if either of you were working from your own center exclusively. Understanding this will ease many of the comparisons we feel compelled to make. Competition is replaced with cooperation, with the ability to make healthy connections with God's other creatures to form the entire tapestry necessary for our world to function.

When you realize you are fearfully, wonderfully, and uniquely made to partner with God in his plan, you won't be afraid of God or pursue unhealthy connections.

Salsa or Applesauce

Maintaining a healthy connection with the father of your children is one of the wisest choices you can make. One of the greatest losses both spouses report upon becoming parents is the loss of connection they feel with each other on many levels.

One of the signs we are feeling this loss can be competition with our spouse as the "other parent." Madison's fifth-grade class was venturing into the deep waters of shark dissection one September morning. The note that came home a few days before said, "If your child would like a piece of the shark to bring home, please send in a clean container and rubbing alcohol." I made note that the memo didn't ask if I actually wanted bits of dead shark in my house, but I poured half a jar of salsa into a bowl to make that container available for the new specimen to come home in, anyway. I felt this was an extra effort on my part at being a good mommy.

The morning of the dissection, Madison and her father were in the kitchen. How the dynamic got set up, I'm not exactly sure. But before I knew it, he was dumping half a jar of applesauce into another half jar of applesauce, cleaning it out for the shark particles that would arrive that afternoon. It was clear to me that my daughter preferred her father's offering to my efforts. I did what any mom would do on churning seas—I went to my bedroom and sulked.

I had a choice regarding my view of this comparison, and I chose to view it as a competition. He won; I lost. Had I not had the good sense a long time ago to marry a marriage-and-family therapist, this could have festered and gotten out of hand. Fortunately, my husband and I have an excellent relationship, and he could show me the error of my ways without me punching him!

Lori Wildenberg, coauthor of *Empowered Parents: Putting Faith First,* tells this story of relational mildew and its impact on her marriage:

> Twenty years is a long time. My husband and I have been married over twenty years. In the course of these two decades we have moved several times. Our marriage is strong. Strong enough to take for granted.
>
> Life can be stressful. In the midst of raising a busy family, time spent dating your spouse is often time that seems to be forgotten. While tending to children and household matters, marriage time seems to sit on the back burner. Gradually, married life becomes disjointed and strained. Feelings of

neglect and frustration build. Communication becomes an information exchange rather than a heart exchange.

Have you experienced this situation? We have. My husband and I spent a significant time apart due to a move from Minnesota to Colorado. We adjusted to the situation and managed life separately, taking care of moving and other details but neglecting one another. We were growing marriage mildew; a fungus that was growing slowly and steadily, causing illness and structural weakness.

Friends, neighbors, family members, coworkers told us we needed to get away together. Apparently they could see what we couldn't. Finally, through sheer frustration, we had an argument. A big one. But a good one. We made the necessary adjustments.

Twenty years is a long time. We're finally learning what God has said all along, "Any city or household divided against itself will not stand" (Matthew 12:25). Division and mildew can slowly creep into our lives if we don't spend time connecting. Marriage time is a necessity for a strong family life, not a luxury. "A strong marriage provides security in the family. Taking time to nurture this relationship empowers parents."[2]

If we truly seek to build a secure and stable home for our children, we need to focus on God and build the marriage. Spending time together, taking time for each other, and managing schedules more efficiently creates a strong foundation. This is the best way to care for our family and for ourselves.

The marital relationship is the most lifelong bond we have. While it is tempting to put it on the back burner when there are so many other people vying for our attention, it is the one relationship that will take us to and through old age, barring accident or divorce. Volumes have been written on this essential connection. As we frame our picture of a sailing mom, we can boil the relationship down to this: The happiest mom is married to someone she both loves and likes, and she mindfully nurtures that relationship first. In a nurturing marriage, it is fair and healthy for you to receive the care you also seek to provide. Tending to the relationship means you are bold and forthcoming with what you need, as well as bold and forthcoming with providing for the other. From this tended relationship comes a sense of co-parenting that can go a long way to alleviating the three choppy Cs (choice, comparisons, competition) and keeping the focus on the household at hand.

There are situations, however, in which a loving marriage is not available to a mother. If you are a mom who has been through a divorce, this positive connection may simply mean you refrain from negative comments about the children's father until the children are old enough to understand the context in which you give those comments. In some cases, choosing to maintain healthy connections means you limit the amount of contact there is between you and another person. At a women's conference I overheard a woman talking at lunch. She fully confessed her need to resolve her bitterness toward her ex-husband because she knew it would set her free to be more healthy for the children they had together. Although admitting it was difficult, she knew she could not continue to harbor the resentment and anger she felt for him without bringing serious issues to her children as they were growing.

True Friends

Choose your friends wisely. Stay away from fools. That's wisdom from the book of Proverbs. But what do foolish friends look like? Proverbs tells us that fools make trouble for others and are ignorant, cynical, careless, and complacent. They don't take counsel. They are dishonest, disloyal, and think they know everything. Fools are headstrong, hardhearted, arrogant, greedy, focused on loot, and restless until they're making trouble. They gossip, engage in idle talk and white lies, and get seduced by sideshows. In short, fools make bad choices, create continuous comparisons, and foster unhealthy competition. The period of your life in which you are raising children is not the time to deal with people or commitments that hang on you, make you feel bad, or make excessive demands on your time or being. Keep a resource file of places you can refer those who are sucking the life out of you and suggest they avail themselves of those resources. A woman's first priority is identifying and choosing the people and Lifesavers that bring health and life. Mark Twain observed, "Keep away from people who try to belittle your ambitions. Small people always do that, but the really great make you feel that you, too, can become great." Greatness is not measured by how much you accomplish, but by how fully and completely you live your Divine Assignment.

I have taken great pleasure in observing groups of women who get together on a regular basis for study, fellowship, and mutual support. The bonds that are forged in these ongoing, long-term friendships are strong and flexible. The traits I have seen in these groups that keep them healthy are:

○ *Delight in diversity.* Although they may have different backgrounds, these women use their differences to learn more about the world, about each other, and about the unique way God works in and through each life.

○ *Laughter through tears.* The women in these friendships have fluid and comfortable expressions of emotion. They feel safe and nurtured no matter what their emotional state.

◯ *Celebration.* In the spirit of noncomparison, these women embrace and celebrate the various achievements, joys, successes, and breakthroughs each other experiences in their lives. Likewise, they show deep concern for times of struggle and offer tangible and relevant help to each other.

◯ *Nonthreatening advice giving.* In these friendships, advice is dispensed with wisdom and respect. Advice is received with wisdom and thoughtful consideration of the counsel given. The friends take care to fully understand the situation before they offer guidance or suggestions.

◯ *Unwavering belief.* These wise friends offer each other a constant in the chaos, an objective trust that the other is growing, developing, and striving to be the most fulfilled creature she can be.

Author and speaker Diana Urban shared with me how she established and maintained healthy connections with friends during the demanding time of having small children and the comfort she still finds now that the kids are older:

> When I was younger, I homeschooled my four sons and ran a home daycare for ten other children, all under six. To say that I had challenging days is an understatement. Sometimes I turned on the radio just to hear adult voices.
>
> One April, I attended a Christian women's conference, and they had a panel discussion. I turned in my written question and waited while the panel read and answered other questions. Finally a panel member opened my slip of paper and read, "Sometimes I feel so overwhelmed with my life and my young children. I want some time to myself, and I feel like

I can't handle any more. What can I do?" The woman answered, "This person really needs to pray through about their attitude. Children are a blessing from God, and you need to be thankful for them." She went on to make other cutting comments, and I wanted to slink from the room. My spirit felt crushed. The only thing that kept me sitting there was that no one knew who had written the question.

I want home determined to make life bearable. Two Bible verses helped me through that time. "Weeping may endure for a night, but joy cometh in the morning" (Psalm 30:5 KJV). I knew that while things might seem bleak at the time, God would help me, and joy would come eventually. "But they that wait upon the LORD shall renew their strength; they shall mount up with wings as eagles; they shall run, and not be weary; and they shall walk, and not faint" (Isaiah 40:31 KJV). The Lord became my strength. He had called my family to serve in a small community, and the strength of knowing that we were where God wanted us carried us through many lonely times and days of hardship.

I developed my main lifeline—the telephone. When the going got rough, I called other mothers and daycare providers. They understood my situation because they lived it daily themselves. The Lord reminds us, "Two are better than one; because they have a good reward for their labour. For if they fall, the one will lift up his fellow: but woe to him that is alone when he falleth; for he hath not another to help him up" (Ecclesiastes 4:9-10 KJV). Whatever our circumstances in life, we need to make connections with other women. Women thrive on the friendships of other women, and we can live and work much more effectively if we find people with whom we can share our sorrows, concerns, and joys.

My days of home daycare are behind me now, and my children are older, but I still need friends. One of my friendships is so deep that we tease each other about being sisters separated at birth. We both have full schedules, but we make time one or twice a week to talk on the phone, and sometimes we have lunch or supper together. Every conversation is an extension of the last one, and we both feel free to say, "I've got to go now," or to call each other any time. If you need a lifeline, try the phone.

One way to maintain healthy friendships is through a delightful tool that has emerged in the last decade called the playgroup. Ann describes hers:

> Our playgroup is a complete blessing from God. There were a total of six moms to begin with—each with one child less than two years old. The actual playgroups were pure craziness at first.
>
> In less than two years, each mom had given birth to her second child. We analyzed each pregnancy down to the wire. We actually discussed that there were not many safer places to go into labor than playgroup!
>
> We talk (actually just try to talk as we are watching the kids) about every pregnancy issue and all things having to do with toddlers. We talk about health (kids, husbands, our own), discipline (kids, husbands, our own!), swing sets, recipes, in-laws, preschool, marriage, marriage counseling, praying...the list is endless!
>
> Because we can never complete an entire conversation during playgroup, we started trying to do a Moms' Dinner every few months. I think it's safe to say that each of our husbands have come to realize the positive influence we have on

each other and therefore are willing to support these outings. Recently we have started to make it Saturday lunch every other month.

Our dream is that this group becomes a weekday coffee club once all the children are in school. Ultimately we are planning a Moms' weekend at the beach. That thought kept me going during this snowy winter.

I cannot even put into words how God has used this group to bless my family and me. My entire journey of motherhood has been given a lifesaving breath of fresh air because of the spirit (I will say Holy Spirit) that these women have shared with me.

We are all blessed with loving, supportive husbands who are great fathers. However, we needed each other, and God knew it! I praise Him for bringing us together!

We know we are in wise friendships when we can experience this thought from Kenny Ausubel: "Each of us has a spark of life inside us, and our highest endeavor ought to be to set off that spark in another."[3] Healthy connections with friends help us maintain our own spark and give us opportunities to bring out the best in others.

Family of Origin

Many mothers cited their siblings when I asked about their favorite connections. Author and photographer Celeste Lilly-Rossman offered this wonderful glimpse into her relationship with her sisters. I wish I were one of them!

I am blessed with four sisters. I have two brothers as well—that is another story, another page, another time. My sisters are always as near as the phone. They have shown over the years that the only words necessary are, "Could you please..." and they set their wheels in motion. Even without the "could you please..." part, they jump in and stay involved in my life without an invitation. They offer to help rather than wait to be asked. They seem to feel that without their involvement the task at hand would be insurmountable. There is a unique beauty in the gift of sisterhood.

I don't believe that it was a parental declaration that all sisters must help each other or is the law of the land where I live. I believe the willingness to help came from the example we saw growing up of our mother helping her mother. It seems that connection is a place of comfort and of trust. I have never doubted that help, for any reason, was more than a dial tone away.

Perhaps it is our diverse and yet similar talents that keep us all interactive. We all have a creative side, yet it had developed in different ways. One can cook, one can wallpaper, one can sew, one can humor, one can be responsible, one can organize, one can nurture, and we all can take a joke. We all dream, and we dream up crazy things, too. We make up things to get involved with just to get our families together. One summer, we made box lunch dinners and tried to outbid each other for the lunch in the most beautiful wrap. Of course, there was no money to bid with—just buckeyes we had gathered at Grandma's house. You can well imagine the laughter in the backyard that day.

It is not all without strife though. Mixing in the in-laws and the children is not always easy. As our families expand there are more and more personalities to deal with and, as we age, our little flaws become more apparent. We all know what it takes for a family to survive. It takes patience, forgiveness, and the effort to try to understand each other. We have differences that won't change and some that change with the coming election. Yet it is the right thing to accept that we are each unique, have a purpose, and voice. A family has to dish out huge helpings of acceptance now and then, as well as potato salad at potlucks.

My sisters act as cheerleaders encouraging my family and me to keep going and to keep pursuing our dreams. And to that I say, "Rah, rah, sisterhood!"

Similarly, I was delighted by Susan's description of her relationship with her mother:

My nearly 80-year-old mother is a great support both with practical assistance and supportive listening. She is not judgmental of my thoughts and is obviously invested with love. We stay in touch by person, phone, and email even though she is only a few miles away. She is an example of true Christian love by her care and selfless support.

It's not surprising with this solid relationship and good modeling that Susan answered this way when I asked her how she keeps her distance from people who are not healthy for her: "I rarely find others who would drag me down, so to speak, as I find something good in most I meet. However, in general, I try to avoid too much negativity in others as that will drag me down. There is a responsibility, however, to seek the good even in our enemies and build upon what we see." Susan also has good balance in her life because part of her vision for herself and her family is that they remain close and interested in each other's lives. She doesn't put priority on others before her family members. In this way, her life is full, rich, and satisfying, and she's not looking to have her emotional needs met at the expense of her vision. She has made good investments into her family, and those relationships are healthy and nourishing.

Our "family of origin" relationships can also give us opportunities to grow healthier through challenges. In families we can't always choose our relationships, but we can make wise and healthy choices about how we will relate to the other people and how we are going to allow them to affect us. The dilemma of a young mother who approached me after I addressed her mom's group at church highlights a circumstance in which all of us find ourselves at one time or another. She is a single-mother with a very young baby. She works part-time to provide for her child while her sister cares for the baby each morning. Through complex family dynamics, this youngest sister in her single mother status has found disfavor with the other sisters. Although they want to be helpful in caring for the baby, they consistently point out all of the youngest sister's flaws, some over which she has little or no control. The young mother who approached me asked me, "As I am to choose healthy connections, should I disconnect from my sister, even though she offers me free childcare? She doesn't help me feel positively about myself, but I sort of need her help so I can work."

At various points in our lives, we are all faced with decisions about connections that may not be healthy for us, but are clearly a part of our lives. At these times we encounter people we can't avoid, so we must make a healthy choice about how we will relate to the other and to ourselves.

While potentially uncomfortable, these positions often lead to a deeper, richer understanding of ourselves. They serve to actually make us stronger and more aware. They serve to draw us closer to God as we seek strength, understanding, and guidance in how to proceed.

My friend Carla understood this kind of decision making in relationship to her mother and the role her mother was to play in Carla's life and the lives of her children.

Things had not always been smooth between Carla and her mother. Some of her mother's own childhood wounds prevented her from bonding with Carla when she was a child. As Carla was growing up, her mother was smothering in many ways and distant and demeaning in others. Carla felt she couldn't trust her mother as she never knew what was going to happen next. They weren't very close, and Carla kept her true feelings about her mother mostly under wraps, understanding that her mother had issues that made her the way she was and not wanting to go further into the murk of her basic uneasiness with her mother.

But by the time grandchildren came along, Carla's mother had gotten some counseling for her own childhood issues and had made some very courageous efforts to become a more open and loving person. Carla's mother was very interested in being actively involved with the grandkids and made efforts to do this in healthy ways.

Carla was conflicted. While she wasn't overly interested in being close to her mother herself, she could understand that her children could benefit from interacting with another generation. She could also understand that her strained relationship with her mother was not a fair or compelling reason to deny her mother the joy of being a grandmother. The mother Carla experienced was not the grandmother her children knew. Carla was faced with the choice of keeping her distance from her mother to keep their relationship healthy and allowing whatever contact her children wanted with their grandmother to keep their relationship healthy. Those levels of contact were not equal.

As she worked through her feelings and the circumstances, Carla became more aware of her own needs as a child, looked for ways to be a more consistent and available mother to her children, spent time trying to objectively understand her mother's world when she was a child, and came to realize that she had plenty of choices as to how she was going to live her life with her understanding of her

Divine Assignment regardless of what she felt she had been given or not given as a child. The choice wasn't black or white—spend time with her mother or not. The choice was black and white and every color in between as she took the opportunity to learn and grow in what appeared to be an uncomfortable choice.

Strength and awareness come from being intentional and clear about why we are making various choices and what we are willing to accept. These choices that involve right *and* wrong, not right *or* wrong, give us unparalleled opportunities to rely on God for all we can see and all we can't see. They place us in the middle of the faith life that is in constant communication with the Holy Spirit as to which way to go when the way doesn't always seem to make sense or to be crystal clear. We trust that we are being guided to choose more life than death, more health than ill.

Choose wisely the cups from which you drink. The only way to do this is to first choose to drink deeply from the cup of fellowship with God through his Spirit. Jesus graphically invited his disciples to stay connected through his object lesson of the vine and the branches in John 15:4:

> Live in me. Make your home in me just as I do in you. In the same way that a branch can't bear grapes by itself but only by being joined to the vine, you can't bear fruit unless you are joined with me. I am the Vine, you are the branches. When you're joined with me and I with you, the relation intimate and organic, the harvest is sure to be abundant (THE MESSAGE).

Part of this abundant harvest will be the ability to make wise choices in maintaining healthy relationships. You will be discerning as you understand your Creator, yourself as his creature, and the best configuration of relationships that will bring you life. Choose wisely.

Search and Rescue

1. *Warm up*—Who are your favorite people in your life at this point? What makes them enjoyable to you?

2. If community is defined as the people who support you and the people you support, who is your main community at this point in your life?

   a. What is your level of involvement with your community?

   b. Would you like more or less involvement at this time?

   c. How can understanding and implementing your Divine Assignment assist you in finding the right level of involvement?

3. When you consider the Myers-Briggs types are you:

   An Introvert or an Extrovert? Thinking or Feeling?

   Sensing or Intuitive? Perceiving or Judging?

4. What temperament is your significant other? Your best friend? Your children? How does knowing there are legitimate differences impact your understanding of the other person and your relationship?

5. When have you needed to make a decision that seemed right and wrong? In the absence of a clear positive outcome, how did you make your choice?

6. Ask God to bring to mind people with whom you enjoy a healthy connection. Ask him to show you what you contribute to their lives and what they contribute to yours. Write out his answer.

7. *Assignment for the upcoming week*—Write and send heartfelt notes to people who make a positive contribution to your life. Thank them for their presence and influence.

14

The Forgiveness Lifesaver

Don't carry a grudge. While you're carrying the
grudge, the other guy's out dancing.

—BUDDY HACKETT

Nothing will drag you to the bottom of the ocean faster than the anchor of unforgiveness. The Forgiveness Lifesaver will help you recognize the places in which you hold an unforgiving spirit. Letting go of this burden will take you a long way to a more buoyant and self-controlled existence.

When you won't forgive, you carry the poundage of pride and the excess of the ego. It's like trying to stay on a course with something constantly whispering in your ear from the sidelines, that annoying little gnat that you have to keep swatting. You are distracted from your purpose and thwarted in your efforts to live a swimmingly abundant life.

As it turns out, the Forgiveness Lifesaver is a lot like the Laughter Lifesaver. Forgiveness is good for your health. In an article entitled "The Healing Power of Forgiveness," Judith Cebula reports:

> Researchers at Stanford University, a leading center for the scientific study of forgiveness, have found that forgiving can lead to:

○ A 20-percent reduction in the physical and emotional symptoms of depression.

○ A 35-percent reduction in the physical symptoms of stress, including dizziness, stomachache, and headache.

○ A 12-percent decrease in feelings of anger.[1]

In addition, the article quotes Reverend Natalia Vonnegut Beck, pastor of Grace Episcopal Church in Muncie, Indiana, and a fellow at Harvard University's Mind/Body Institute, saying, "We're learning that the act of forgiving someone who has hurt you or finally forgiving yourself can have a profound impact on blood pressure, depression, and overall feelings of wellness."

One of the things I have always appreciated about the instructions of Jesus is that they are so practical and loving in caring for our whole person, not just our spiritual natures. Jesus gave such loving guidance because he knew it would enable us to love God with all of our heart, soul, mind, and *strength*—the renewed strength we gain from forgiving.

In addition to the health benefits of forgiving, the spiritual benefits include the ability to understand that we ourselves are forgiven. Did you ever wonder why Jesus said, "Unless you forgive others, your heavenly Father won't forgive you" (see Matthew 6:15)? When I contemplated this, I wondered how it was I had so much power that I could sway God's actions by what I did, or I wondered about a God who seemed to be playing childish games. But when we reflect on Jesus' Divine Assignment, "I have come that you might have life and have it more abundantly," and that everything Jesus said and did was to bring that about, I realize that he was saying that when I refuse to forgive, or even to be willing to try, I disconnect myself from God—I put a block between myself and God. We don't have the wonderful flow of energy and Holy Spirit between us when my heart is stiff, and I won't embrace that I am made in his image and, therefore, my best nature longs to be like him—forgiving. Jesus' words in Matthew were not a finger-wagging, tongue-clicking warning against being a bad person. They were another example of how to stay connected to God for our maximum wholeness. As always, God seems to be thinking of us first.

Forgiveness is not always rational. It is rarely a movement of the mind only. Forgiveness involves our heart, soul, mind, and strength. It is a matter of the will and the heart. It involves our entire being.

What Do We Forgive?

We forgive in two categories. First, we forgive people (ourselves included) for actual transgressions they have done that hurt us either through their intentional action or by their neglecting to do something. This type of forgiveness is not saying the transgression is okay. Friend, colleague, and author Dr. Tom Walker once told me that in his family, when they are about the business of pardoning one another, they say "I forgive you." They are careful not to say, "It's okay," because it may very well not be okay. It's not okay to hit other people, to call them names, to hurt their bodies or spirits through willful or neglectful thoughtlessness or malice. Forgiveness frees yourself from carrying the burden of revenge or licking the wounds that keep you from living life to the fullest.

The second category of forgiveness is often more powerful because it is more hidden. Sometimes we find ourselves having to forgive someone just because they haven't lived up to our expectations or they are not doing things the way we want them to be done. There is no malice or neglect, just a difference between what we want and what we're getting. These are imagined or perceived transgressions, lacks, or lapses in being considerate.

The power of these imagined transgressions is that we can tell ourselves in our heads, "I know I shouldn't be mad/disappointed/ hurt over this because they are just being who they are and living their own lives," but in our hearts and emotions we are holding on to what we want to be that isn't. It's hard to bring these to the surface because someone could say, "You're just being silly" or "You have no right to think that." But we do nonetheless, and until we can forgive the imagined or perceived transgression, it will have a potent hold on our ability to be free and happy, and to joyfully relate to others.

Forgiving Ourselves

There are three types of forgiveness that are particularly helpful to mothers who seek to live full, rich, and meaningful lives. The first is forgiving ourselves for not being someone else.

At one point I was having difficulty at my workplace. My advisor identified that I was feeling overshadowed by the man who had previously filled the church position I now held. Everywhere I turned, it seemed, people were saying, "Well, when Joe (not his real name) was here, this is how he did it." Or, "You should have seen how Joe handled a situation like this." Joe knew a lot, cared a lot, made people laugh a lot, and made people think a lot. Joe was a real pain in my side. One day during a coaching session, my advisor said with tongue in cheek, "Why don't you just forgive yourself for not being Joe?" What a goofy thought. But it was a great piece of advice.

I went home and through my tears I wrote a hundred times on a piece of paper, "I forgive myself for not being Joe." Rationally I knew I wasn't Joe, I should never compare myself to others, and I brought my own unique set of gifts and graces to the situation to which God had called me. But emotionally, I still felt inadequate by comparison and routinely judged inferior by those around me.

This can happen in any relationship, not just work situations. Maybe you took over being the chairperson of a big event only to find that the person before you walked on water and had a killer recipe for chicken salad all at the same time. Perhaps you were the sibling who didn't measure up to another. You might be the stepmother who will just never compare to a mother who has been lost through death or divorce.

Forgiving ourselves shatters the opportunity for comparisons to take hold. Forgiving ourselves for not being someone else embraces that we are indeed different from any other creature and that we have been given distinct Divine Assignments.

The second type of forgiveness is for things we actually do—wrongs we commit but that are accidental in nature.

Dawn faced a situation in which she found she had to forgive herself for something she actually did, but didn't mean to do. I'll let her tell the story:

When a pediatrician explains that you have possibly poisoned your child, accident or not it is a scary thing. Carlee was almost one, and she had come down with a virus. She could not hold down anything except fluids, particularly Pedialyte. After the illness, she would only drink Pedialyte and not eat any solid foods. Being a first-time mom, I figured as long as she was getting nutrition, she would be okay.

As the days went by, Carlee began to get more and more sluggish. This behavior was unlike her and became a concern for me. I called her pediatrician's office and described the situation and her symptoms. They instructed me to bring her right over. Upon arrival and after a very thorough examination, Nurse Practitioner Rogers wanted to do some testing to see if Carlee had electrolyte poisoning! Unbeknownst to me, the first-time mom, too many electrolytes in anyone's body—much less a small child's—can be a very bad thing. After some blood tests were taken, we were sent home to wait for the results.

The only vivid thing I remember on the drive home is saying to God, "I know that Carlee is a gift from you. She doesn't belong to me, and if this is all the time that you have given her to us, then thank you for that time."

I am not a super-saint by any means. I fall on my face and break the Father's heart more than I would like to admit, but our loving, amazing Father was working through a not-so-bright, first-time mom.

Dawn goes on to explain that through the experience, Carlee's grandmother was touched to find out more about God through Dawn's example of forgiving herself and the strength she found in her relationship with God.

The third and hardest type of forgiveness to extend to ourselves is for things that we have done or left undone, that were indeed intentional. We meant to do it, we made a conscious choice to do something, or we didn't stop ourselves from doing it.

My friend Carolyn tells of choices she needs to make at this point in her life, how those choices are affecting her, and what she feels she needs to forgive and why:

> I've found that I most need to forgive myself. I have a tendency to be something of a perfectionist. My life right now is chaos, and I can't afford to be a perfectionist. I have a special-needs child, and my husband and I are struggling to just get through day-to-day life. Everywhere I look, there's a big pile of guilt facing me. The house is piled with things that need to be taken care of somehow…bills to be paid, stuff to put

away, laundry to do, dog hair to sweep. There are household maintenance projects that we do just to the point of making it livable, and then we are forced to move on to the next one to put out that fire. Consequently, we have unfinished projects mocking us everywhere. We haven't even put the pictures back up from a remodeling project last year!

The reason all of this is so hard is we have a four-year-old son who has special needs. He takes extra time to work with and take care of. I have a seventeen-month-old daughter who, despite my best efforts, is taking a backseat to my son's needs. With my perfectionistic nature, it's a constant struggle not to be overcome with guilt at the state of the house and the state of my mothering.

Our children are our priority. We have to choose to forgive ourselves about all the things that remain undone. We have to choose to forgive ourselves for not being the "perfect" parents. Yes, I should be reading more to my daughter. Yes, it would be great if I could do neat little crafts with my son, but my life just doesn't work that way right now. I do the laundry I need to do and in the middle of folding it, I stop to dance to music with my children. There's a hole in my bathroom wall that needs to be fixed because of the leaky shower, but I was able to give my son physical therapy twice this week.

Sometimes it still gets us down, but my husband and I have to forgive ourselves for not having the organized, peaceful home we dreamed about. Our kids are getting what they need. We can't assuage our guilt by working hard on holes in the wall and in so doing, neglect the greater needs of our children. We have our priorities straight. We just need to remind ourselves of that and forgive ourselves for the chaos in the meantime.

Distinct from what Carolyn is talking about are the times when we make intentional choices to do something mean or hurtful, or we don't stop ourselves in the act. Have you ever been to the point where you have just had it? Everyone and everything is pushing a button and nobody seems to care at all that you have feelings, tolerance levels, and a need to not be the ever-ready solution to everyone's needs and demands. An incident or a person pushes you too far and you lose it, striking back in a way that causes a little red flag to go up in your "you better not do this" territory, but you are simply in such need of an emotional release and a sense of being validated as a person that you do it anyway. It may be a physical or verbal transgression, and you know in the back of your mind it's not right. Afterward you are overcome with guilt, and you diligently ask for forgiveness. These intentional choices are often the most difficult to forgive—but forgive yourself you must or you'll sink to the bottom of the ocean.

A very powerful piece of forgiving ourselves is the ability to allow others to forgive us, too. Writer and speaker Diana Taylor shared this moving story of forgiveness with me:

> After struggling in my marriage to an alcoholic for twenty-one years, I filed for divorce. My grounds were adultery. With all that went on, we became a truly dysfunctional family.
>
> Due to the circumstances in my marriage, I had no confidence in myself, and though I was a Christian and attending church, I was walking with one foot in church and one foot in the world. Bad relationships with people outside of my family were harming my relationship with my children and adding to their pain.
>
> One day the scripture "when we confess our sins, he is faithful and just to forgive our sins and cleanse us from all

unrighteousness" touched my heart. I knew I needed to make a change in my life and needed God's help. When the Lord finally got through to me, I was overcome with remorse and shame. Instead of looking to the deep needs of my children, I had only seen my own needs and pain.

After praying for wisdom and strength and with my heart in hand, I sat down with each of my children individually and confessed that what I had done was wrong. I asked for their forgiveness for not being the mother they needed me to be. I told them how much I loved them and that I wanted to be different, that from now on I wanted to walk in God's ways.

To my surprise and relief, each one of them listened and with tears in their eyes extended their forgiveness. They in turn asked forgiveness for the way they had treated me and for the things they had done. In each of those times, God's love covered our sins and brought restoration.

As my daughter once said, "Mom, we always knew two things: that you loved us and that we could always come home."

In Asia there is a saying, "He who cannot forgive, burns the bridge over which he too must someday pass." We all face that bridge at one time or another. Thank God for his forgiveness that enables us to forgive ourselves, and then, in turn, forgive others.

Forgiving Our Past

For people who don't seem to carry the pain of flagrant and chronic abuse from childhood, yet still carry uneasiness or unhappiness about their family of origin, there are two potent words: toxic cookies. What are toxic cookies? They are little morsels that looked innocent enough when we were growing up, but we have since understood them to get in the way of the full and abundant life that we are to live at our creative best. These little cookies were rules, worldviews, guilt trips, or other input we couldn't or "shouldn't" argue with when we were children. Toxic cookies could come from relatives, coaches, teachers, church leaders, or any other person or group who had authority in our lives. Toxic cookies are about everything from work habits to sexuality, from physical appearance to relationships. Some of the most toxic cookies are about God.

Some toxic cookies have a well-intentioned moral behind them. "Don't get too full of yourself." "Don't argue with me. I'm the boss." "Put yourself last, and you'll be happy." "You should be ashamed of yourself."

Some toxic cookies are built-in shields to family dignity. "If you're going to embarrass yourself, do it at home." "Don't do anything you don't want your mother to know about."

Some toxic cookies carry honest parental concern. "We will always be here for you to provide whatever you need." "Don't wear your hair like that. It makes you look goofy."

Some toxic cookies reveal a deep-seated pain in the one who was feeding them to us. "It isn't any use for you to try to get an education. Women aren't supposed to do that." "No matter how hard you work, there's always someone who didn't do as much getting something better."

Some toxic cookies are simply theories on life and the way things work. "Life is black and white, right or wrong. That's the way it is." "There you have it. Trust a man with your heart, and just see what happens." "Once that's gone, there isn't any more."

Some toxic cookies are downright lethal. "You will never amount to a hill of beans." "Your father left us because he didn't like you." "I abuse you because you aren't a human being worthy of love, dignity, or respect."

Now, as one woman put it in a retreat I led, "I didn't get toxic cookies, I got toxic meatloaf!" You may have an entire catalog of toxic cookie incidences in your life. You may discover you don't want to face your toxic cookies or meatloaf alone. Perhaps they are so toxic that they threaten to destroy you. Don't let whatever shame you have as a result of these cookies keep you from seeking genuine and professional help in taking on these joy-stealing life-robbers.

Toxic cookies are very powerful impediments to you understanding and pursuing your Divine Assignment. Because toxic cookies are only the view of someone else, we have to examine them and make choices about them for ourselves. Looking at these cookies can be daunting and painful. It can also feel like we are blaming or criticizing others in our past (which can come from a toxic cookie itself). The healing that comes from looking at and dealing with toxic cookies is in understanding several things:

○ The people who fed us toxic cookies were dealing with their own issues, and their anger, disappointment, or inferiority spilled over onto us. We were usually children who did not deserve that input, but we were the closest and least-threatening people in their lives.

○ Toxic cookies are only opinions and worldviews expressed by others. As children, we believe that what happens in our family is what happens in every family, as strange as our family may have seemed. To look at these toxic cookies as grown-ups helps us understand that the whole world didn't and doesn't think like our family of origin, and we have options about the worldviews we take as our own.

○ God stands between us and those who fed us toxic cookies. Many times we eat the cookies as children because we don't want to see the authority figure suffer alone. We also want to make it better for them. Understanding the framework of another's toxic cookies, and our own limitations to make things better, enables us to let God take care of that person. God stands ready to heal that other person should he or she want to be healed. You are released from that responsibility.

When we look at toxic cookies, we are freed and enabled to see negative, joy-stealing input as separate from ourselves, and then we can choose the input we want for ourselves as we go forward. Just as the food we eat may influence our health but it is never "us," toxic cookies may have influenced us but they are not who we are in our God-given essence.

Examining and eliminating our toxic cookies enables us to look at the type of cookies we feed to others—our children included—and helps us make better communication decisions.

Good Friday and Easter are all about examining and eliminating our toxic cookies. In my coaching practice, when I talk with mothers about their toxic cookies, I have them envision a plate of these deadly, sweet-looking morsels. I ask them to identify the cookies from their past. As they do this, I encourage them to invite Jesus to the table to eat the cookies. That's Good Friday. As Jesus was taking on all sin—past, present, and future—he was taking on the pain and brokenness that leads to toxic cookies. He ate them. Every last one.

Then I ask these mothers to envision Christ rising on Easter morning and walking to the place where the plate was sitting. Christ picks up the plate and tosses it like a Frisbee into the air, never to be seen again. It's gone. No more cookies, no more plate. You are free.

You are free to forgive all those who put those cookies in your life. You are free to make your own decisions about how you choose to see the world. You are free to decide you want your relationships to go another way. You are free to swim rather than to sink. Letting Jesus handle the toxic cookies is like breaking through the surface after being underwater for so long. If you haven't actually experienced that yourself, think of a time you have seen someone on television or in a movie who has been submerged under water for a length of time without life support. They have one goal: Get to the surface for some air. When they break through to oxygen, their whole being takes on a different tone. They are free, they are back to normal, they can live.

Forgiving Our Current Family

The biggest thing I needed to forgive my children for was keeping me from sleeping. I was mad at God about that, too. Sometimes, when the kids were really little, I would flop back down in my bed in the middle of the night after yet another feeding, crying (the kids, not me), changing diapers, or just basic disruption and say, "God, you really must hate me to have given me these children who won't let me sleep." None of it made any sense, but I was angry with all of them just the same.

What I had totally out of whack was my expectation of what small children are like and what they should do for me to maintain my comfort level. I found I had to constantly forgive my children for embarrassing me, inconveniencing me, making me unable to finish all that I wanted to finish. In short, I had to forgive them for being children who needed a mother.

In my relationship with my husband, the things I need to forgive are usually those things that a) reflect skewed expectations or b) hurt my feelings. In both cases, these things could be alleviated by me becoming more aligned with my Divine Assignment and in my relationship with God. Don't misunderstand me, I'm not talking about a pious stance that hides behind religion saying everything is all right. I'm talking about understanding myself in the context of how God feels about me and letting that be the first place I go to get my nourishment and self-worth.

For example, if I have expectations that David violates, I have to ask myself where those expectations came from, are they realistic, did David do something wrong in violating them, and did he even know I had those expectations. There are some things we have every right to expect such as faithfulness, respect, a safe environment, and responsible provision. When those are violated it is time for serious talk, repair, and forgiveness. Very serious decisions must be made in those cases. In the cases of shoes being left out, no roses every Friday, an afternoon of paying attention to the golf match rather than to me, or being late to dinner, I need to assess the gravity of the situation and run through the questions I stated earlier.

When it comes to hurt feelings, I need to ask myself if he meant to, is he touching off a toxic cookie from my past, are there ways that my own self-esteem is more easily bruised in this particular arena, and how soon I'll be able to get back at him. Just kidding on the last one. But I have found that when it comes to anyone hurting my feelings, I have to ask myself where I am in my own heart with how I feel about myself. I am not saying we excuse people who are malicious, rude, thoughtless, or egocentric, but I do always need to check my own question, "Why did that hurt me?"

I was completely amazed at the weight that was lifted off my shoulders the first time one of my kids told me they hated me. It's a harsh thing to say, no doubt. But I realized that I could live through it, that *I* didn't hate me, and that they were honestly expressing a feeling that would be fleeting. Now when they get mad at me, I tell them, "It isn't the first time. It won't be the last. I love me and I love you, and you can hate me without damaging our relationship as far as I'm concerned." The difference is in my expectations. If I expect my children or husband to never be upset with me, or to never express that upsetness, I will be in for a shock every time it happens. My realistic expectations and self-esteem make it much easier for me to forgive.

Forgiving Others

DenaRae Carlock highlights how keenly forgiveness and happiness are linked.

"If momma ain't happy, ain't nobody happy!" is one of my favorite sayings. It always elicits a smile, making me chuckle a little on the inside—probably because it rings so true in most of the young families I know.

I have thought a lot about this saying lately, and I've decided that while I chuckle at this saying, if "momma" is in a perpetual state of unhappiness then "momma" needs to get to the bottom of what is bothering her.

As I look back at my own life, I realize now one of the things that keeps me in a state of perpetual unhappiness is when I harbor unforgiveness towards others, whether for words spoken to me or actions against me. At times I have had a real struggle being able to release the unforgiveness and to let go of the hurt I have felt. Yet this struggle and release is mandatory in order to be a more effective mom or stepmom.

When my husband and I were newlyweds, it was a very frustrating time for me. Added to the normal first year of marriage anxiety, I had inherited my husband's two sons from his first marriage. Although they have always been easy for me to deal with, their mother, at times, has been a completely different story. It took me several years to realize some of the mistakes I was making with these two boys.

One day I realized that I was becoming irritable not only to them, but at the thought of their very presence in my house. I realized that my feelings stemmed from the fact that I was extremely irritated with their mother (for something she had either said or done), and that they personally had done nothing to me. At that point I knew I needed to separate my feelings for my two stepsons and my ill feelings toward their mother. I had to make the distinction so the boys wouldn't be caught in the crossfire. As I began to separate the boys and my feelings for their mother, it was easier to have the boys in my household and easier to work on forgiveness issues where their mother was concerned.

It has only been through time and conscious effort that I have been better able to separate my feelings of unforgiveness toward the people who have offended me and the innocent bystanders who live under my roof. I have come to realize that if I am in turmoil the entire house is in turmoil, and that turmoil is not a very good place to spend your childhood.

I now realize that God alone is able to help break this cycle. As I look back over my life, I wonder how different every aspect could have been if I really believed Jesus when He said He would never leave me or forsake me. That He meant He would be there for me in the everyday things that happen to me, and not just while I was walking out the Great Commission. Jesus' intention was, and still is, that when someone hurts us, if we could just imagine Him standing right behind us, ready for us to throw that unforgiveness ball over our backs to Him, He is standing there ready to catch it and throw it away. He wants to help us become lighter on the inside so that we can become better moms.

Forgiving God

As I noted earlier in this chapter, not all forgiveness seems to be rational. One of the most irrational relationships of forgiveness is the one we have with God.

Have you ever been so mad at God but you didn't want to express it? Maybe you thought God would get mad back, and then you would really be up a creek. Maybe you thought God wouldn't want to listen to you if you were angry. Maybe you thought it wouldn't do any good anyway because God is God, and he will do whatever he wants to whether you like it or not. In any of these cases, check for a hearty dose of toxic cookies on your childhood plate somewhere.

The good news regarding being angry with God and needing to forgive God is that God can take it. He is not the person in your past who cut you off or made you feel guilty for being angry. God is not threatened by your anger. He's not seeking to retaliate. God breaks the mold of anyone you have ever known before. His primary desire is not to put you in your place, but to place you in his arms.

The poetic section of Scripture known as the book of Psalms is full of conversations with God called "laments." In a lament, the writer pours out all kinds of feelings to God. Anger, confusion, despair come spilling out. The most frequently asked question is "Why?" "Why, O LORD, do you stand far off? Why do you hide yourself in times of trouble?" (Psalm 10:1). "My God, my God, why have you forsaken me? Why are you so far from saving me, so far from the words of my groaning?" (22:1). "I say to God my Rock, 'Why have you forgotten me? Why must I go about mourning, oppressed by the enemy?'" (42:9). "You are God my stronghold.

Why have you rejected me?" (43:2) "Why do you hide your face and forget our misery and oppression?" (44:24). "Why have you rejected us forever, O God? Why does your anger smolder against the sheep of your pasture?" (74:1). "Why, O Lord, do you reject me and hide your face from me?" (88:14).

If you have ever felt abandoned by God, if you have ever wondered why the things that have come into your life are there, if you have ever been angry for being ignored, you are not alone. God gave us the psalmists and their psalms to show that we are safe in expressing these emotions.

For what are you angry with God? Where do you think you have been shortchanged or overloaded? What loss have you experienced? What burdensome addition have you been given? What relationship or experience has given you grounds to question God's goodness?

We live in an era of court television, where every case that is made has to have hard evidence, rock-solid facts, and airtight reasoning to be successfully prosecuted. We wouldn't dare enter into litigation without having a good argument. But God doesn't live in court television land, and he has no desire for the relationship we have with him to be adversarial. Rational or not, airtight or not, we can take our disappointments, hurts, and feelings of being unjustly treated to God. He doesn't demand ironclad facts. He offers a listening presence and a deeper assurance that we are loved despite appearances. The chasm between us and God will never be bridged if we don't forgive God and let God forgive us.

First Corinthians Forgiveness

As my husband and I prepared for a Valentine's Day presentation we were giving at a Sweetheart Banquet in a local church, we outlined four points we believe are basic to a thriving Christian marriage. My assignment was to present the point of forgiveness. (God does things like that to me all the time. He says, "Robin, this is an area in which you need to grow, so I would like you to do a presentation on it!" God has a funny sense of humor that way.)

I try to be big on application, on asking people to envision what a new learning will actually look like in their lives. Process and theory are entertaining, but it's the real-life application of a principle that makes all the difference. So I asked myself, "What does forgiveness look like as it is literally applied to life?"

One of the reasons forgiveness is so difficult is that it makes us feel vulnerable. We are opened to the possibility that the other person will take advantage of us. We may be seen as weak for being the one to want reconciliation. We may appear to be a sap for tolerating the bad behavior of another. To be available to the potential of forgiveness, we need to have a shift in our thinking that enables us to see forgiveness as an empowered state, not a weakened state.

The most powerful force on earth is love. Our ability to forgive without fear is rooted in love. And where do many of us turn when we need a refresher course on this topic of love? First Corinthians 13:

> Love is patient, love is kind. It does not envy, it does not boast, it is not proud. It is not rude, it is not self-seeking, it is not easily angered, it keeps no record of wrongs. Love does not delight in evil but rejoices with the truth. It always protects, always trusts, always hopes, always perseveres. Love never fails (verses 4-8).

What if we took the word "forgiveness" and placed it temporarily in the spot that "love" holds? "Forgiveness is patient, forgiveness is kind." This puts us back into a healthy alignment with God, who knows that asking us to forgive is asking us to take on a task beyond our ability. God's call is often like that. As John Ortberg notes in *If*

You Want to Walk on Water, You've Got to Get Out of the Boat, a call from God is frequently marked by feelings of fear and frustration. Why? Because God never wants us to depend on ourselves and our own resources to accomplish something. And forgiveness is an accomplishment!

Forgiveness can only protect, trust, hope, and persevere as it relates to the strength we draw by staying true to the ultimate call of focusing on and being loved by God first. Fear and frustration in forgiveness come when we are focused on ourselves or on other people. When we are empowered by our own purpose first, we are much less susceptible to the opinion of others.

Forgiveness as a Foundation

Our entire life together as Christians is based on the practice of forgiveness—first God forgiving us, and then us forgiving each other. That forgiveness is based in a deep desire to not be separated and estranged. God offers us forgiveness because he knows we will be happiest bathed in his love and acceptance. There is no substitute for him. Then God asks us to keep the lines of love and acceptance as open with others as possible. I have a wise friend who asks herself on a continual basis, "Would I rather be 'right' or be 'reconciled'?" When we forgive, we cut the anchor of "rightness" from around our necks and live harmoniously with God, with others, and with ourselves. We experience peace.

Search and Rescue

1. *Warm up*—What does it mean to you to be forgiven?

2. What are some examples of real transgressions that need to be forgiven? What are some examples of imagined transgressions that need to be forgiven?

3. For what do you need to forgive yourself?

4. What are the toxic cookies of your past? Whom do you need to forgive to rid yourself of their power?

5. What does it mean to you that Jesus ate the last of the toxic cookies and tossed out the plate as well?

6. For what do you need to forgive your children or your spouse?

7. For what do you need to forgive God?

8. Write a prayer to God about someone you need to forgive. Ask to be reminded of the forgiveness you have received and for God to help you wherever you are in the process of forgiving the person, realizing it may not happen all at once. Write out his answer.

9. *Assignment for the upcoming week*—The topic of forgiveness can be heavy. Treat yourself to some ice cream.

15

The Yes and No Lifesaver

Simply let your "Yes" be "Yes," and your "No," "No."

—MATTHEW 5:37

I had good intentions, really I did. As I weighed the request and examined its merits, I thought, *It will give me a chance to stretch and grow, to prepare new material. I might even meet some new people who will want to use my professional services in the future.* The very fact that I had to think on it for quite a while should have been a red flag.

But the deeper I got into preparation for teaching the three-week Wednesday night session on fasting at my church, the crankier I got and the more resentful I was that I had said yes to the invitation to teach.

Was the invitation a bad invitation? Certainly not. Was the topic something that didn't really matter to the world? No, of course not. Had I said yes for the wrong reasons and was I working outside my Divine Assignment at that point in time? Absolutely.

Knowing how to authentically say yes and say no takes great sensitivity to the Holy Spirit because only in that dynamic and intimate relationship are we going to get the true answers we need. There are all kinds of reasons to say yes when we should say no. What if someone else won't do it? What if they don't like me because

I say no? What if the task doesn't get done as well by someone else as it could be done by me? What if nobody asks me to do anything again (which might actually be a blessing)? What if I miss a great opportunity just because I can't fit this into my life right now? What if my children are shunned because I won't get involved in this way? I don't have anything else to do, so I may as well do this (now *that's* a rare one, I'll admit!). The true bottom line question is: "What if I'm overcome by guilt and anxiety if I say no?"

We mothers are prime candidates for being asked to do everything from baking a plate of brownies for the upcoming school bake sale to chairing the arts festival in the community. We are a very capable lot—able to juggle many and varied tasks and responsibilities. But sometimes we simply take on things that are not ours to take on. Then the balance is disrupted, the boat capsizes, and we're splashing around, overwhelmed again.

The Wisdom of Two-Year-Olds

Our two-year-olds have it all over us when it comes to getting to the heart of a matter. They love to ask "Why?" And with good reason. It's short, simple, focused on the present and wants to be answered immediately and thoroughly. We can learn a great deal from our two-year-olds and employ this one little word to change our family stress level forever.

My husband, the therapist, says in the counseling community there are those who are uncomfortable with the word "why." He said it makes people defensive when you ask them that question. Here we go back to tone of voice and intent of question. If we are indeed demanding and accusatory in our questioning, we will elicit defensiveness as the other person feels attacked. And that "other" may be ourselves. But if the question comes gently, with the intent of true exploration and caring, the question is healthy and leads to greater understanding and the potential to make necessary changes.

Continually ask yourself "Why?" Why are we doing this activity, this sport, this lesson, or this group? On what kingdom are we focused? Jesus pointed out that unless we become like little children, we cannot become participants in the kingdom of God. As we practice the use of "Why?" we help keep ourselves focused on the right kingdom and on the one who rules and overrules all of our circumstances.

We use this question whenever we are faced with a demand on our resources. When first using this practice, it seems to slow down everything we do. It can feel cumbersome to ask, "Why am I spending this money?" "Why am I saying yes to this request for my time?" "Why did I agree to use my talent in this way?" But it is an investment that pays off in the long run. Have you ever returned something because it was an impulse purchase? Have you ever wished you had said no to a particular assignment? Did you ever feel you had wasted your time or skill on a project? While asking why seems to slow you down at first, it actually saves time in the long run. It also helps you more authentically identify your uniqueness.

Being open to the "why" question gives the Holy Spirit time and space to work in our lives through prayer, conversation with wise people, and assessment of our true call. The word "why" gives us the opportunity to pause and consider an option. It gives us breathing room to make a careful assessment of our resources and to forecast the impact of saying yes or no. Asking why gives us the space we need to examine our motives.

And that's why I have always said mothering is not for wimps. It takes strong, centered women to honestly assess motives. It takes strong, centered women to choose sanity over popularity. It takes strong, centered women to choose substance over appearance. It takes strong, centered women to recognize the particular genius of their own children and not clutter their lives with lots of other activities just because everyone else is. Say yes and no for the right reasons. Some potentially dangerous reasons for saying yes to any request for your resources are:

- Everyone else is.

- It will help my child get ahead.

- It will help me get ahead.

- We need something to fill up our time.

- I'll feel guilty if I say no.

Any motive that can be traced to satisfying a comparison or a competition holds a risky reason for participating.

Second, our two-year-olds are highly adept at saying no. Therein lies the clue as to why it's so hard for us to say no at times. How did others respond to you when you said no as a child? Did they seek your point of view? Probably not. They may have told you to do it anyway. They may have shut you out if you said no. They may have made you feel guilty for not doing things their way. While I'm certainly no advocate of letting two-year-olds rule the family agenda with their yeses and nos, I think we can learn a lesson from them in their unreserved ability to know what they want and to take a stand.

My friend Beth has discerned her Divine Assignment to be Hospitality. She uses this Yes and No Lifesaver to help her set the limits she wants for herself and her family.

Saying yes or no with conviction is easy for me, although I say it with a quiet voice because many moms are so much more giving than I of their time. I, Miss Hospitality, feel convicted that my family and their peace must come first. While I occasionally say yes to something that will cause some chaos in our lives, I more often don't. Having quit a job, some years back now, that threw my life, and so theirs, into disarray and stress, I watch carefully that this doesn't happen again. I pray to feel God's guidance as to what I should say yes to, and then I follow it. Not surprisingly, whatever I say yes to always, either immediately or eventually, leads to growth in my life, and growth and joy in our family. One day I expect, when kiddies are out of my nest, my yes/no criteria might change. I'll see what God says!

It should come as no surprise that Beth is one of those mothers I mentioned in Chapter 1 when I said I looked around and discovered there were mothers who were content and confident. She has always been one to remove herself, with quiet dignity, from the fray of comparisons and competition. She models that saying no isn't comparable to being irresponsible. She says no in a healthy, appropriate way that ensures she has the energy for what matters most to her.

Diana Urban offered this about saying yes and no with conviction:

I am no challenged. I suffer from all of the reasons why people say yes when they should say no. How have I learned to control my tongue when it wants to spout, "Yes, I'll do that"? First, I clarify exactly what is being asked of me. If it's something in which I'm not interested, I say no immediately and thank them for the opportunity. I try to offer alternatives if I can think of anyone else who might be qualified. If I am interested in what is offered, I tell the person I'll think about it. That gives me time to review my schedule and goals to see if I actually want to plan time for that event or responsibility. I prefer not to disclose my reasons for saying no because people may want to argue my refusal. If appropriate, I simply say I have another appointment, even if it's with my bubble bath and a novel. Taking time to relax and set goals keeps me sane. My goals help me evaluate what is important to me and enable me to say yes only to tasks that will further my aims.

Say yes because you see the opportunity for your child and your family to explore another facet of purpose as it's unfolding in each of you.

Say yes because you firmly believe that it's an expression of the Divine Assignments you and your family have identified.

Say yes because it broadens your horizons without thinning your energy and enthusiasm for life.

Say yes because the opportunity highlights and celebrates the uniqueness of your family.

Play a game with yourself called "Drop the Banana." I'm sure you've heard the story about capturing monkeys by using a box that is designed so the monkey can slip his hand through the slats to grab the banana inside, but when the banana is in the monkey's fist, he can't pull it back out. He is faced with a choice, keep the prize and stay trapped or drop the banana and be free. What outwardly driven motives or prizes are keeping you trapped in certain situations when you could drop the pretense and be free?

When It Involves Our Own Family

Some of the hardest people to hold to the yes/no line are our family members. Speaker Cheryl Jakubowski describes it as "staying the course." She and her husband had a firm grasp of what they believed to be their Divine Assignment regarding their daughters. Although the going was rough sailing at times, they found that foundation helped them be consistent in saying yes and no with conviction. Here is Cheryl's story:

> I remember the day our daughter Kerry thanked us for setting limits for her as if it were yesterday. The sky was clear, we were standing in the parking lot outside of church. She had just returned from a weeklong summer church camp where she was in charge of a cabin of fourth-grade girls. It was her last summer at home before going to college to realize her lifelong dream of becoming a teacher.
>
> We are a blended family. Boy, do I hate that term! The reality of raising someone else's children part time or full time very seldom is smooth like anything blended. I equate it more to the first time I tried to make gravy from scratch. Lumpy, yet full of flavor, the ingredients being what made it taste so good, but you needed to steer clear of the lumps. Well, as a family we had taken our lumps, and being blended was not easily accomplished. One of the biggest "lumps" we encountered in our new family was the fact that we seemed to be the strictest parents in the world.
>
> Kerry and Amy came to live with us full time when they were thirteen and eleven years old. Having been weekend parents for six years, we were suddenly in the role of being a family 24/7. Expectations were high that we would naturally evolve into a well-run family. Of course, to make that happen took a lot more than evolution. It took hard work and conviction.
>
> Having two young women in our home brought up many issues for both my husband and myself. He was still involved

with being the "fun" dad that many noncustodial parents become. The fear of losing their affections was great, so he was the full-time entertainment committee. I, on the other hand, became the disciplinarian, the wicked stepmother so familiar to the Disney generation.

Dating was not allowed unless in a group before the age of sixteen. Church group outings were allowed, also sports activities, band, drama club, and any other extracurricular activity offered by the school. As working parents, my husband and I expected the girls to come home each day and check in by phone. Unless we authorized it beforehand, no girlfriends were allowed to visit. Boys were never to come into the house unless my husband and I were present. Parties were never attended unless we spoke to the parents first. Many times after receiving the type of answers we did from the parents hosting, the girls were not allowed to attend the party.

What kept us focused on holding our principles while keeping the girls as safe as possible was the overwhelming desire to help them become whole adults. We wanted them to be adults who made the right choices for themselves, or even in making bad choices would know they were responsible for the outcome. Being unpopular for our views in their eyes as well as some of our peers was something we decided to live with.

Proverbs 19:18 states: "Discipline your son, for in that there is hope; do not be a willing party to his death." Death comes in many forms to a young woman who makes the wrong choices, and it was our purpose to help keep them safe by offering discipline.

We held fast to the idea that it was only for a season. The girls would grow and mature, they would leave home. We would be left with a life of our own, wanting to be able to look ourselves in the eye knowing we did all we could to protect them. Did we ever expect their appreciation for a job well done? No, not really. They resented the fact they did not get to participate in many of the activities their friends did. We had to thicken our skin to push through it even when, as parents, we didn't always agree with one another. We decided a united front was best.

So after years of crying, heartache, and resolving to keep on setting limits, we heard the words we never expected from our daughter Kerry. Stepping down from the camp bus she said, "Thank you for protecting me and for setting limits. After a week of 24-hour-per-day responsibility for those children, I now understand you set limits out of love for me."

I don't remember feeling proud of myself for doing the right thing as a parent. What I do remember feeling was a sense of awe that God would love each of us enough to validate us as his children. He had entrusted his children, Kerry and Amy, to our care for their upbringing. As adult parents we were still God's children, and Kerry's validation of our parenting was an affirmation from him.

Kerry's maturity still stands her in good stead today. She is in her sixth year of teaching middle school, and she is much loved as a teacher. Our youngest, Amy, is a high school guidance counselor. She is still shocked to see the latitude some parents allow their children and the consequences the children must pay.

Remembering the end result, the prize of protected daughters kept us on track as we enforced our house rules. Seeing the results of our vigilance, as parents, was priceless. Being unpopular with our children for a season was worth the sacrifice. Our relationships with our daughters as adults are full of warmth, care, and compassion. I believe it would not be so without being willing to protect them by setting rules as they matured.

Proverbs 15:32 says, "He who ignores discipline despises himself, but whoever heeds correction gains understanding."

This story would not have been possible if Cheryl and her husband were not convinced of their God-given identity and purpose with these young women. These parents envisioned what they wanted their daughters' lives to look like as responsible, caring women who would make good choices. Cheryl and her husband's Divine Assignment and their vision for the future gave them the compass point they needed to stay on the path.

A Matter of Trust

Saying yes and saying no with conviction is essentially a matter of trust. We need to trust that we are worthwhile in this world as we follow our convictions. We need to trust that all that truly needs to be done will be done by the intricate plan of God, which we don't control. We need to trust that our families will be provided for by the loving hand of God and not by what we engineer by way of social status or over-involvement to ensure their place in this world. We need to trust that all things will work together for good, even if the waters get a little choppy as we stand our ground. What are the elements of this kind of trust?

○ *Unlace the running shoes.* If we are in constant motion, we are numb to the moving of the Spirit. It is hard to be aware of God working in our lives if we are overboard with activity.

○ *Give up the vise grip.* Let go. Let go of your agendas and your perceptions of how things should be. Let go of your expectations of what life ought to be and how it will come about. It helps to clutch as little as possible, allowing God the room to do what God does best—make all things work together for good for those who love him and are living out their Divine Assignments.

○ *Trust.* As we are trusting God, we need to be aware that we can honestly trust ourselves, too. We need to trust that the still small voice speaking to us is indeed the Spirit working through our own hearts to ensure we have the right focus and the right answer at the appropriate time. The more we are aligned with God through intention, the more we will be sensitive to his prompting. As we have been created in the image of God and seek to embrace that identity as our own, we can trust ourselves as God's agents.

○ *Recognize our place in the river.* We don't chart the course of the river. Nobody ever really asked us to. But sometimes we feel like we have to be the water, the banks, the trees on the bank, and all the little fishies, too. Recognize that you are part of the river, but not the whole thing. The beauty of the scene doesn't depend entirely on you. Know your part and live it with joy.

○ *Get out of your own way.* As Esther Armstrong and Dale Stitt put it in their wonderful newsletter *Journey into Freedom* (March 2003), "Give God some wiggle room. While this is (of course) a lifetime task, we can begin through prayer and meditation to turn our lives over to the care of God, as we understand God. In so doing we can begin to operate out of our center instead of our egos."

The ultimate role model for saying yes and saying no with conviction is Jesus Christ. Let's look carefully at his example in Matthew 4:1-11:

> Then Jesus was led by the Spirit into the desert to be tempted by the devil. After fasting forty days and forty nights, he was hungry. The tempter came to him and said, "If you are the Son of God, tell these stones to become bread." Jesus answered, "It is written: 'Man does not live on bread alone, but on every word that comes from the mouth of God.'" Then the devil took him to the holy city and had him stand on the highest point of the temple. "If you are the Son of God," he said, "throw yourself down. For it is written: 'He will command his angels concerning you, and they will lift you up in their hands, so that you will not strike your foot against a stone.'" Jesus answered him, "It is also written: 'Do not put the Lord your God to the test.'" Again, the devil took him to a very high mountain and showed him all the kingdoms of the world and their splendor. "All this I will give you," he said, "if you will bow down and worship me." Jesus said to him, "Away from me, Satan! For it is written: 'Worship the Lord your God, and serve him only.'" Then the devil left him, and angels came and attended him.

Satan appeared to tempt Jesus with food, riches, and prestige. What Satan really wanted was not for Jesus to fall for any of his traps, but for Jesus to betray the essence of why he was sent to earth. In each of the three instances of temptation, Satan tried to make Jesus deny his identity. Satan tried to make him say yes when Jesus should say no and no when he should say yes. Jesus, aware of the consequences of betraying his identity and purpose, said yes and no with confidence.

You can, too. Live from your Divine Assignment, and trust God with the outcome.

Search and Rescue

1. *Warm up*—Name a time when you said yes and you felt peaceful about it. Name a time when you said yes and you should have said no. How did you feel about that?

2. Reclaim and restate your Divine Assignment. How can your Divine Assignment help you make better decisions about your yeses and nos?

3. When you say yes or no to your kids, can you articulate why? Do you have a vision for the character you want for them to exhibit in their lives? How are your choices and your yeses and nos helping to shape them in these ways?

4. Is there a situation right now in which you need to rethink a yes or a no and do something about it?

5. Where do you need to use the wise words of the two-year-old? As you go through your calendar and your checkbook, make a list of what you find and the answers you find to the question "Why?" Why do you spend the money you spend? Why do you do the things you do? Are those reasons in keeping with your Divine Assignment and your vision for your life?

6. Ask God where you need to let your yes be yes and your no be no. Ask him to show you places where you might be stuck, and places where he might want you to go. Write out his answer.

7. *Assignment for the upcoming week*—Run every request for your time, talent, and money through the filter of your Divine Assignment. What happens when you do this?

16

The Celebrate Uniqueness Lifesaver

Just do what you do best.

—RED AUERBACH

The last sentence of the article grabbed my attention. I applauded it initially because it is a philosophy I learned through intensive soul-searching. Then the true impact burrowed in. The sentence read, "You're enough. Period."

In "Doing Less Helps Child in Long Run," Samantha Campbell highlighted an emerging approach to parenting explored in a book called *Trees Make the Best Mobiles*, by Jessica Teich. The author urges parents to allow children of all ages downtime to explore their world in their way. She advocates that we be there for our children, but not with them every moment. She challenges the norm of constant stimulation offered by everything from flash cards in cribs to the full menu of classes and lessons our older children struggle to regularly maintain. Her encouragement is to allow children to live life alongside you.[1]

"You're enough. Period." I felt like crying for all the women I have met in the past years who don't, for one reason or another, believe that. I felt like crying for all the years I had believed the toxic cookie that said I wasn't enough, that somehow God had made an endless string of mistakes by creating me to be who I was, where I was, and what I was.

We constantly ingest advertising specifically geared to fuel our sense of inadequacy in everything from the way we look to the way we cook and from the car we drive to the house we own. A poll of 618 women found that 50 percent of us find nagging defects in our body when we look in the mirror. On top of that, 27 percent rarely like what we see. When asked what the cause of this dissatisfaction could be, 67 percent respond "impossibly beautiful media images." We keep up facades in our group meetings and gatherings. In situations when our children are truly challenged mentally, physically, or emotionally, we think it's our fault or downright unfair that they aren't as perfect as other children. When we can't be first, we simply don't want to play.

Yet the pesky feeling of inadequacy persists even when we are perceived by ourselves or others to be number one. Even when we have reached the top or our children have achieved greatness, even when we have acquired everything we thought we should have to be the envy of our neighbors and friends, there comes a point when we realize that we can be first and still not be enough.

One small shift in thinking can produce profound transformation.

When you are living the Celebrate Uniqueness Lifesaver, you realize that being enough is far more desirable than being first. When you know in your heart that you are enough, the peace, contentedness, and satisfaction obliterate the striving and frustration of choice, comparison, and competition. It's like realizing you have been watching a soap opera on television while sitting in the middle of the California redwoods.

The Kingdom of Celebration

The kingdom of God is like a wedding feast (Matthew 22), a waiting father (Luke 15), a woman finding a lost coin (Luke 15), and a shepherd finding a lost sheep (Luke 15). When we celebrate, we are participating in the very fiber of the kingdom, or "your kingdom come…on earth as it is in heaven." All of these stories of Jesus illustrated celebrations of authenticity, relationships, and connection.

What does it mean to celebrate? It is to recognize and acknowledge something with glee. On our life journey, it's a chance to look at where we've been, what we've learned, what we anticipate. It's like pitching a big tent on the trail, setting up a beautiful spread of food, putting on the music, and enjoying the scenery because you have had a good, long hike.

To celebrate uniqueness, we must live in the present. Christ gave sound advice to mothers when he strongly suggested that we live in the present and savor the moment. I can almost see the wry smile on his face when he said we all have enough trouble for the day without borrowing other trouble (Matthew 6:34). When you are indeed living in the moment, you will find the surprises, the celebratory moments, that are unique to that moment.

When you are uncluttered and focused, you will feel more like celebrating. Celebrating comes more naturally if we have realistic expectations and learn to be content with the present. Don't wait for things to be perfect to celebrate! Kids get their teeth brushed this morning? Celebrate! None of the white laundry turned pink in the last load? Celebrate! Somebody give you a hug? Celebrate! Did you laugh when you could have yelled? Celebrate! Did you remember your Divine Assignment today and have an opportunity to live it out? Celebrate!

When you celebrate the uniqueness of your family, you help kids realize that they don't have to compete. They don't have to compare. Your family has a culture completely to itself. You don't have to put other people down—they simply have a different culture. When Madison is invited to a sleepover at someone's house, she comes home with stories of how that family did things differently. They ate different food, had different bedtime rituals, and played different games. As long as nothing immoral, dangerous, or illegal was going on, we talk about those differences as being distinguishing elements of that family. What are the distinguishing elements of your family, and of each member of your family?

Distinguishing Family Features

Patti and her family have established a way to celebrate they refer to as "calling out the best" in each other. They believe God has made each of them different from the other. They believe there is a purpose and a plan for those differences. They believe that if they are watching for those differences and naming the good those differences bring to the world, they will be better equipped to go into their school, office, and community to call out the best in others. They celebrate their uniqueness in their approach to developing as individuals and as a family unit.

I asked my friend Karen how her family is unique and how they celebrate that uniqueness. She said,

> I never gave this much thought before, but I think we are unique. We are a single-parent family of two that continues to share a closeness and friendship that a lot of families don't have the time to nurture. We make it a point to know what is going on with the other person. We talk to one another and really take the time to listen to what the other person has

to say. I am not saying that it is always a rosy picture or that tempers don't flare, but we do make it a point to communicate with one another. I guess we celebrate this uniqueness by having evenings out, just the two of us—no other family or friends—just a night for us to be together, whether it be something as simple as going out to dinner or a movie or an ice cream, or something special that we share together.

Your family's uniqueness can be described in interests and activities. Nancy says her girls make lists of activities they want to do like "roller blade" or "go out for pancakes." They post them on the refrigerator, and they check off the items as they do them. This keeps Nancy focused on what they really want to do.

Other families find their uniqueness in lifestyles or particular challenges. One mother said,

> It's hard not to be a unique family when your child is adopted and diabetic, though we work very hard to make both of these "nonissues." We are truly unique in our old-fashioned lifestyle. We hire out far less chores at our house than most families. Also, we eat dinner every night together with no television on. We live within our means and save to buy what we want and need. We don't take tons of lessons and have lots of activities. As our son gets older, we want him to be involved, but not at the price of being a kid. My husband and I are both just small-town Indiana kids. We don't know how to live any other way.

Linda finds her family is distinguished by their sense of humor. They celebrate by playing pranks on each other. Recently she and her preschooler hid a purple snake under Daddy's dinner plate. Her family loves to laugh.

Your family may be unique in the way you communicate. Nancy felt her family always had a knack for knowing what each other was thinking. Donnae liked that her family had spontaneity and levity built into everything they did. Both of these mothers now have empty nests and are enjoying the strands of their own families showing up again in the families of their children. They celebrate that their children are choosing to extend the family legacy in their kids and grandkids.

Celebration and Gratitude

The Celebrate Uniqueness Lifesaver is compelling because it is essentially embedded in gratitude. When we celebrate, we are thankful. We are thankful we have found one another. We are thankful God has given us a purpose in our lives. We are appreciative of the many gifts God has given to us. We acknowledge our indebtedness to God for the wonder of life in our family. Deep happiness comes from the practice of gratitude.

An ancient Greek proverb states, "Wonder is the beginning of wisdom." Take time to marvel in the wonder of your family. Know that there is no other family configuration like yours—so celebrate the uniqueness of your family!

Search and Rescue

1. *Warm up*—Write a word picture of a terrific party. Describe the details such as food, reason for the party, decorations, and people in attendance.

2. In what ways do you understand yourself to be "enough"? In what ways do you feel you are not "enough"?

3. Why is it better to be enough rather than be number one?

4. What are three distinguishing characteristics of each member of your family? What are three distinguishing characteristics of your family as a whole?

5. What does your family like to celebrate? How does your family like to celebrate?

6. What would you say is your family's Divine Assignment? How can you use all of the passions, skills, talents, and interests represented in your family to help bring that Divine Assignment to reality in your life and the lives of those around you? This is part of your uniqueness as a family.

7. Ask God to show you how your family is unique and the things you can be celebrating. Write out his answer.

8. *Assignment for the upcoming week*—Keep a celebration chart in a prominent place this week, and encourage your family to write down things they want to celebrate.

17

The Gratitude Lifesaver

Thankfulness is the mother of joy.

—M.J. RYAN

I really wasn't very grateful as a mother of young children. Everything irritated me. I wasn't getting any of the sleep I deserved. I couldn't paint my nails like I thought I should be able to. Since I had left the work world, I didn't have the discretionary income I wanted to have to keep pace with my neighbors and the others in my social and church circles. I was cranky and self-absorbed. Life sure wasn't turning out the way I had envisioned.

By worldly standards, I gave up a lot when I became a mother. I gave up a second income, a big house, an ability to run in some social circles, vacations, and sleep. I gave up my superior edge of having more than some people have. I gave up outward things that gave me my identity at that point in my life. The return on my new investment didn't bring up much gratitude in me.

Furthermore, I didn't want to be grateful because I believed that would signal to God that I was okay with my new circumstances, and I wasn't. I didn't want God to get the impression that in my gratitude I was content with the way things were. I thought if I stayed miserable I could somehow manipulate God into giving me what I wanted in my external surroundings to satisfy my material and ego wants. What a shock for me to begin to see the same behaviors in my two-year-old daughter! I was behaving like a clueless, egocentric child, and God wasn't falling for it.

The worst part is that I still had so much. I just didn't have as much as I wanted, especially sleep. (Do you see a theme running through this section?) Since I didn't have everything I wanted, I wasn't going to be grateful for what I did have. That means I was actually worse than a two-year-old, who doesn't know any better. I was acting like a thirteen-year-old who does know better, but isn't going to give in.

My biggest problem was I didn't believe I could be grateful until things were just the way I wanted them. And in my case, those "things" had a lot to do with my house, my clothes, my trips, my children's toys, and my experiences. I believed that I needed to wait to be joy-filled and happy until my outer circumstances were just right. I was in the mind-set that many baby boomers have. I was "entitled" to things because I'm basically a good person who is also kind of smart and cute. As a young adult, I wanted to live in the same lifestyle I had enjoyed as an older teenager, when my parents were providing me with everything I desired. Somewhere along the line I had missed the lesson that when it came time for me to be independent, I was to provide for myself—and whatever level of income my husband and I earned would be the means within which we would have to live. I've never been very astute in economics.

We can learn a great deal about how God feels about us and interacts with us as we seek to mold our kids into good and gracious creatures. What's one of the first graces we teach our children? We teach them to say "please" and "thank you." We hope they will see that relationship always comes before material wants, and the true joy in giving and receiving is found in the heart of the other person.

God had mercy on me and didn't send me to too many time-out sessions before he allowed me to come to the point of "please" and "thank you" in my relationship with him. God just let me live with myself and my self-pity until I had come to the end of my desire to live a thankless, joyless life. More importantly, he was patient and possibly humored as I struggled to understand that my relationship with him is always the most precious gift. He allowed me to understand the awe in the fact that I'm even invited to say "please" and "thank you" to the Creator of the universe and the profound Lover of my heart. My circumstances didn't change right away, but my outlook and appreciation for all that I had changed a little each day. Maybe it's because I was getting more sleep, too!

I began to understand firsthand what Max Lucado describes in his book *Traveling Light:*

> Paul says that "godliness with contentment is great gain" (1 Timothy 6:6). When we surrender to God the cumbersome sack of discontent, we don't just give up something, we gain something. God replaces it with a lightweight, tailor-made, sorrow-resistant attaché of gratitude. What will you gain with contentment? You may gain your marriage. You may gain precious hours with your children. You may gain your self-respect. You may gain joy. You may gain the faith to say, "The Lord is my shepherd; I shall not want."[1]

Benefits of Gratitude

One of the foremost benefits of gratitude is it frees us from the prison of self-focus. In other words, when we feel the urge to be thankful, we usually want to be thankful to someone. As Christina Rossetti said, "Were there no God, we should be in this glorious world with grateful hearts and no one to thank." The more times we are grateful, the more drawn we are to the Giver rather than the gifts.

Gratitude has been described as a natural upper. When we are grateful, we lose the blinders or tunnel vision that we can experience through focusing on what's wrong with or missing in our lives. We gain some energy—another reason to be grateful. We see more around us that is worth noting with thankfulness—a reason to be grateful. We can actually attract others of a like mind to us because they like what they see in us—another reason to be grateful.

Physically, we do ourselves a great service when we practice gratitude. It seems nearly impossible to worry and be grateful at the same time. All of us know what a toll worry takes on us, from stomach problems to insomnia. When we worry, our bodies produce chemicals that are really only necessary for acute situations of fear. But worry is simply prolonged and permanent fear, and those chemicals eat away at our bodies, leaving us depleted and sick. Gratitude can heal our bodies as well as our souls.

As mothers, one of the most powerful benefits of gratitude is that it teaches our children to be grateful. There I was grousing about all the lacks in my life, and then I was expecting my children to have nice attitudes and to appreciate all that I did for them. I was consumed by the adult version of the "gimmes," but annoyed by the pint-sized version when I took my kids on our frequent excursions to yet another superstore. I would get so put out with their complaints that I nearly patented a phrase: "Some people live in station wagons." I loved to throw that one out when I felt the kids needed a bit of perspective. Only trouble was, I had to listen to myself saying it and look in the mirror to see what my kids were actually seeing all along. After I began to cultivate an "attitude of gratitude," I could see my kids becoming less whiny, as well.

Perhaps the most important reason to practice gratitude is that it heals our souls. To illustrate this, here's a modern paraphrase of a wonderful story of healing and gratitude found in Luke 17:14-16.

It seems that one day a group of ten mothers was gathered outside the nearest gym. Watching lots of other women go in and out, they were huddled at the door commiserating that they were not worthy to go into the facility because of various physical flaws like their hips, tummies, thighs, noses, chins, or upper arms.

They heard a commotion down the way of the strip mall and realized that the Great Physician, whom they had heard was touring their town, was getting out of a van surrounded by his disciples and other followers. This Physician was renowned for his ability to heal bodies and level the playing field for the "haves" and the "have-nots." He was noted in the region as someone who could help outcast people like them.

Figuring they were already shunned and calling out in a public place couldn't possibly hurt their social standing any further, they joined their voices together to yell for the Physician to come to where they were. They knew, just on intuition and reputation, that if he simply spoke the word, their flaws would be righted and they would no longer be embarrassed outsiders. They would be able to join the beautiful people.

The Physician did come to them, and true to his reputation of mercy and healing, said to them, "Go show yourselves to the physical trainers inside who will declare you to be the right size, the right shape, and the right weight." And as they departed his presence, each of the ten had their flaws corrected. They were beautiful.

The last of the ten to go into the gym paused at the door and turned around to approach the Physician. When she came close, she took his hand, held it to her newly beautified cheek, and knelt. Looking up into his face, fully engaged in eye contact, she said, "Thank you."

Still holding her hand, the Physician looked to his followers who had observed the whole thing. "Didn't I just beautify ten of them?" And to the one who still knelt in gratitude he said, "Go your way, your gratitude has made you whole."

Why did the Physician go the extra step and say that additional phrase? Didn't she already have all that she wanted? Wasn't she now able to join the rest of society because she was beautiful and fit in? But in that moment, something happened in her heart. At the Physician's pronouncement, "Your gratitude has made you whole" she understood that anything the Physician could do for her on a physical level would never truly make her feel complete. It was only in the intimate connection between the two of them that she could be free from comparisons and competitions. The other nine who had entered the gym before her, even though certifiably beautiful, were deep into the comparison game all over again even as she knelt and found peace.

Hindrances to Gratitude

A very heavy anchor that can drag us to the bottom of the Cs of choice, comparisons, and competition is perfectionism. As we saw in Chapter 3, perfectionism can keep us from discovering and living our Divine Assignments. It can also keep us from experiencing the joy and beauty of a grateful spirit.

Some of us picked up the toxic cookie in childhood that if we did everything perfectly, we would be all right. The challenge is that life is a little unpredictable, and, even more annoying, we're not always in control. Life can get chaotic. People don't always behave as we think they will or should. Circumstances are often altered from the "norm."

Perfectionism can keep us from the very thing that will offer us respite from its relentless push—an open and grateful heart. "Because perfectionism is born of a sense of inadequacy, of lack, an attitude of gratitude counteracts it by tapping us into the experience of abundance. Gratitude makes our world feel complete and right. When we feel the fullness of gratitude, we accept life just as it is—however messy, complicated, and drawn-outside-the-lines that may be."[2]

Unrealistic expectations can keep us from expressing gratitude as well. When we have these expectations, we are not able to receive and enjoy what simply is. We only see what needs more, or fixing, or healing. We only see that what we wanted to have happen didn't.

Worry is another enemy of gratitude. What is worry usually focused on? Either something in the past that has gone wrong or that we fear will catch up with us or something in the future that we want to control but can't. Living solidly in the present moment tills the fertile soil of gratitude.

Applications of Gratitude

We can start to reach for and grab the Gratitude Lifesaver no matter where we are. It may take some practice and a softening of our hearts (and preconceived expectations) to bring it to reality. Beth gives a wonderful example of this kind of transformation.

> When Kelsey was a baby, she was difficult. Crying nonstop, eating nonstop…exhausting me and really upsetting me. My mother-in-law was up helping and said, every time I was

around the two of them, that it was a privilege to take care of her granddaughter (as that granddaughter was screaming in her ear!). She told me to say that over and over again, day after day, and I would come to believe it. I did, and it worked. Some time later, I started thanking God every morning for the day to come and every evening for the day that I had experienced. I expressed my gratitude for good health and good friends. It didn't take long for me to truly feel that gratitude. It was the repetition and the awareness of gratitude that has made me truly feel grateful. And, difficult as this is to admit, I think aging also helps gratitude! There is wisdom in realizing the wonder and gift of our lives. My gratitude is always to God and to those He has given me.

Gratitude gave Beth a new perspective. Gratitude also gives us the energy to stay engaged in a situation that might be taxing. Author and motivational speaker Sally Philbrick Smith tells of a time when she was grateful for the Word of God speaking directly to her, and the difference it made in her attitude:

The noise level of 27 people in a five-room farmhouse (including two bedrooms and one bathroom) would challenge the level of a band concert.

The women spent two-and-one-half hours in the kitchen preparing and cleaning up the evening meal. When we finally finished, I announced that the kitchen was closed until breakfast the next morning.

Two hours later, the flow of children started back into the kitchen for evening snacks. Anger welled up within me. At bedtime I was still so mad that there was no way I could relax and get to sleep. I picked up the Bible and said, "Father, I can't go to sleep in this frame of mind. Show me something in your Word to calm me."

God led me to Psalm 143:7-8. " 'Answer me quickly, O LORD; my spirit fails. Do not hide your face from me or I will be like those who go down to the pit.' (This evening has been the pits, Lord). 'Let the morning bring me word of your unfailing love, for I have put my trust in you.' "

"That's beautiful, Lord. It is just what I need for a failing spirit. Oh, how I want your unfailing love. I want tomorrow to be different. I need you to show me the way to walk."

One of the beauties of Sally's story is that she was completely in touch with her feelings. She knew she was angry and had reached her limit. She didn't gloss over that fact. And she also knew to look to God for a word that would soothe her. She chose to be receptive in spite of her situation. She kept her heart open to the Almighty, even though her circumstances were driving her crazy. This led to something God could give her, and her heart was then grateful. When we are open and honest, God can move more effectively and quickly through our lives, and we can experience gratitude more easily.

Gratitude is a choice. Another one of the mothers that I looked to as a model of contentment and confidence was my friend Susan. On gratitude, she shared this with me: "My underlying goal is to maintain gratitude for God in all things. I continually choose to see what is working in my life as I become older and wiser, and I give thanks for this. I am so grateful to God first, and then gratitude extends outward from there." Susan stays aware of her life, even with two young children, and keeps making choices to be grateful for what is.

Jeanne shared a wonderful practice she and her family implement every year. It's called the Thankful Box: "For many years, in

November, I set on our kitchen table a boutique-size tissue box covered in fall fabric, with a pad of notepaper and pen next to it. Until Thanksgiving Day, family members add notes telling what they are thankful for. On Thanksgiving night, when I serve pie, we spill the box's contents and read them to each other. Some years we went through tough times. A father and favorite uncle died ten days apart. Another year, we were nearly killed by a drunk driver, and ten days later a parent was diagnosed with cancer. Yet we could praise God for getting us through the tough times. Of course, praises were easy: our pastor, our warm home on a cold night, the first snowfall, a good mark on a test, an unexpected job to meet a bill. Many families practice a time of sharing one thing for which they're thankful just before the Thanksgiving meal. But by having a month to think about our blessings and fill that little box, we are reminded again of God's compassion and help in many areas of our lives."

The Gratitude Lifesaver is last on the list, but certainly not last in importance. By grabbing onto this Lifesaver, we are pulled closer to the ship S.S. Sanity because we are pulled nearer to the heart of God. That's where our true sanity is found.

Search and Rescue

1. *Warm up*—Write down ten things you are grateful for at this very moment.

2. What is holding you back from feeling and expressing complete gratitude? How long are you willing to wait for the situation to be changed to your specifications? What are the benefits of gratitude that you're missing out on right now?

3. Respond to the reflection by St. Paul in Philippians 4:12: "I have learned the secret of being content in any and every situation, whether well fed or hungry, whether living in plenty or in want." What do you think the secret is?

4. How have the advertising world, the media, or magazines influenced your ability to be grateful? What standards do they set? Are those standards the ones by which you want to live your life?

5. When have you experienced unexpected gratitude, and how did it affect your outlook on a situation? To whom were you grateful and for what?

6. Ask God to show you where you could receive more joy in life by having your heart more open to his Spirit. Write out his answer.

7. *Assignment for the upcoming week*—Spend some time pondering the difference between being grateful *in* everything and being grateful *for* everything.

Epilogue

L ike any new skill, becoming a sailing mother takes practice. Few of us are proficient at something the very first time we do it. In fact, it's a toxic cookie to think we have to be great at something the very first time. That keeps many of us from trying anything new at all. But we don't practice so we can become perfect in the traditional sense of the word. We practice so we can become perfect in the definition we found in Chapter 3: to become more fully who we are, to fill the purpose of our birth, and to keep our focus on God. To do that, we need to keep in perspective what we want in the end and who we are in the process. We need to set our sights as we scan the horizon from the railing of the S.S. Sanity.

One of my favorite verses in the Old Testament is Proverbs 31:28: "Her children arise and call her blessed." As someone once said, "I would be content if my children would just arise!" But as I started giving the Proverbs verse more thought and became familiar with the translation of the word "blessed" to mean "happy," I found epiphany.

This verse doesn't mean I will have to wait another decade or two to see if my kids will bless me, will truly appreciate what I've done for them. It speaks to how my kids will remember me!

Will my children remember me as "happy"? I'm sure they will remember me as others of the seven dwarves—namely Sleepy, Grumpy, and Dopey. Perhaps they'll even remember that I was "Doc." I may have even been "Bashful" at times. But will they remember me as "Happy"?

Happy is not just about always being cheerful and smiling, although, when genuine, that can't hurt moms or kids. Happy is a state of being that is characterized by peacefulness and a soul satisfaction that comes only from being in tune with and playing to the audience of One—the Creator. This deep happiness is remembered by kids who have grown and have appreciation for the way they were raised. It comes from a woman who has made a careful exploration of who she is and creatively lives the life she has been given. This deep contentment comes from having confidence in one's decisions, shunning distracting comparisons, and dismantling destructive competitions.

The good new is it's never too late. God rules and overrules. "If anyone is in Christ, he is a new creation" (2 Corinthians 5:17). If you feel you weren't a great mom or weren't acting from your Divine Assignment, or if you think you have damaged your kids, it's not too late. Go to them if they're older and confess and make amends. If they're younger, simply practice your new skills of working from your Divine Assignment.

I want to leave you with this final thought, a benediction of sorts. If you copy this and put it somewhere that is consistently in front of your eyes and remind yourself of four little thoughts, when you see it, you will sail through the roughest waters and stay on board your ship.

What are the four thoughts that I desire you hold dear? They are the answers found in this scripture:

May the God of hope fill you will all joy and peace as you trust in him, so that you may overflow with hope by the power of the Holy Spirit (Romans 15:13).

1. Where does hope originate? Stay connected to the source.

2. With how much joy and peace does God want to fill you? God is not stingy. He never has been; he never will be.

3. What is the measure of how much hope you will have? A trickle just won't do!

4. What's your power source? Just like radio waves are constantly around us and we have to set the dial to pick up what we desire, the Holy Spirit is always around and in us. We need to set the dial for maximum reception.

So stand tall on the deck of your ship, secure in the knowledge that when you encounter the choppy Cs and if you do get thrown overboard from time to time, you will not sink. You know the safety and power of the Divine Assignment Lifeboat and the 12 essential Lifesavers. Most importantly, you know the heart of God who sent you this precious rescue equipment. You are never alone. You are never adrift. Sail on.

Search and Rescue

1. *Warm up*—Can you name all seven dwarves from *Snow White*? Which of the seven dwarves are you?

2. For what do you want to be remembered as a mother?

3. As you ponder the benediction from Romans 15:13 answer the following questions:

   a. What would it look like in your life for you to truly believe that God is a God of hope?

   b. Where do you most need to have peace and joy in your life? Where do you already have peace and joy? What do you think needs to happen for you to have *all* peace and joy?

   c. What would it feel like to overflow with hope? What would be the effect on you? What would be the effect on your family? On your friends? On your community?

   d. What do you need to do to more effectively set your "radio dial" to pick up, enjoy, and utilize the power of the Holy Spirit? Where do you currently have static? When have you had clear reception before? What did it feel like?

4. Write a prayer to God about what you have learned, what you are grateful for, what you want help in changing, and how you feel about him. Write out his answer.

5. *Assignment for the upcoming week*—Give yourself a big hug. You have worked hard. Now take a few moments to stretch out on a deck chair, soak up a few rays, and sip some lemonade.

Notes for Discussion Leaders

When we are in conversation with others, what matters most is how we treat one another, not where we come down on an issue. We each bring a beautiful, searching, and experienced voice to the dialog. As a preacher once said, "When Christ comes to a conversation, he doesn't take sides—he takes over!" So for maximum growth, be involved with and listen carefully to your diverse group. Remember guidance from James 3:17: "But the wisdom that comes from heaven is first of all pure; then peace-loving, considerate, submissive, full of mercy and good fruit, impartial and sincere." Talk together in the presence of God's Holy Spirit. Enter your discussions prayerfully, expectantly, openly, and wisely. Here are some further suggestions:

○ The "leader" should be the person who keeps the discussion moving. She does not need particular biblical or psychological knowledge or skill. She should have read the book chapter and Search and Rescue ahead of time to make herself familiar with the material.

○ Allow at least 60 minutes for each discussion. Good discussion includes time of thoughtful silence. If you are done before 60 minutes has passed, do not feel compelled to stay in your seats until the time is up! In the same vein, if you need more than one week to look at a particular topic, don't rush through the material just to hold to a schedule. Let the Holy Spirit guide your time together.

○ Keep a box of colored pencils, markers, or crayons close to your discussion area. Have note cards so people can write to influential mothers in their lives.

○ As your group members feel led, begin each time with a recap of the previous week's assignment and how implementing it impacted their lives.

○ Some groups like to begin and end in prayer. Some take prayer requests and keep a journal of God's hand moving through situations and lives. Follow whatever pattern is most growth-producing in your group. Now may be the time to talk through those patterns to discern if they indeed are the ones your group wants to continue. Be bold in trying something new!

Notes

Chapter One—Why Is Mommy Splashing Around?

1. Os Guinness, *The Call: Finding and Fulfilling Your Central Purpose in Life* (Nashville: Word Publishing, 1998), p. 176.

Chapter Three—The Divine Assignment

1. William Barclay, *The Gospel of Matthew, Volume One* (Edinburgh: Saint Andrew Press), pp. 177-78.

2. John Ortberg, *If You Want to Walk on Water, You've Got to Get Out of the Boat* (Grand Rapids, MI: Zondervan, 2001), p. 81.

3. Guinness, *The Call,* p. 43.

Chapter Four—Discovering Your Divine Assignment

1. Frederick Buechner, *Wishful Thinking: A Seeker's ABC* (San Francisco: HarperSanFrancisco, 1993), pp. 118-19.

Chapter Five—A View from the Bow

1. Charles Swindoll, source unknown.

Chapter Seven—The Self-Care Lifesaver

1. Statistics are from Gail Kopecky Wallace and Ann Pleshette Murphy, "Moms Don't Get No Respect," *Family Circle,* May 21, 2002, p. 60.

2. Dallas Willard, *The Divine Conspiracy: Rediscovering Our Hidden Life in God* (San Francisco: HarperSanFrancisco, 1998), p. 15.

3. Henry Cloud and John Townsend, *12 "Christian" Beliefs That Can Drive You Crazy: Relief from False Assumptions* (Grand Rapids, MI: Zondervan Publishing House, 1995), pp. 15-16.

Chapter Ten—The Play Lifesaver

1. Ann Pleshette Murphy, "Mom Know-How," *Family Circle,* May 21, 2002, p. 40.

2. Mary Dixon Lebeau, "The Serious Side of Play," *Indy's Child,* June 30, 2002, p. 32.

3. Conrad Hyers, quoted in *The Lift Your Spirits Quote Book* (New York: Portland House, 2001), p. 33.

Chapter Eleven—The Touch Lifesaver

1. Nitya Lacroix, *The Scented Touch* (London: Anness Publishing Limited, 1999), p. 43.

Chapter Twelve—The Recording Lifesaver

1. Buechner, *Wishful Thinking,* p. 101.

2. Frederick Buechner, *Listening to Your Life* (San Francisco: HarperSanFrancisco, 1992), p. 277.

Chapter Thirteen—The Healthy Connections Lifesaver

1. Betty Southard and Marita Littauer, *Come as You Are: How Your Personality Shapes Your Relationship with God* (Minneapolis: Bethany House Publishers, 1999), p. 19, based on 500 surveys from people across the nation.

2. Lori Wildenberg and Becky Danielson, *Empowered Parents* (Gainesville, FL: Synergy Publishers, 2003), pp. 102-03.

3. Kenny Ausubel, quoted in *Lift Your Spirits Quote Book,* p. 41.

Chapter Fourteen—The Forgiveness Lifesaver

1. Judith Cebula, "The Healing Power of Forgiveness," *The Indianapolis Star,* March 27, 2003.

Chapter Sixteen—The Celebration Uniqueness Lifesaver

1. Samantha Campbell, "Doing Less Helps Child in Long Run," *Indianapolis Star,* January 9, 2002.

Chapter Seventeen—The Gratitude Lifesaver

1. Max Lucado, *Traveling Light* (Nashville: Word Publishing Group, 2001), p. 34.

2. M.J. Ryan, *Attitudes of Gratitude* (Berkeley, CA: Conari Press, 1999), p. 30.

Suggested Reading

Barnhill, Julie Ann. *She's Gonna Blow!: Real Help for Moms Dealing with Anger.* Eugene, OR: Harvest House Publishers, 2001.

Bolles, Richard N. *How to Find Your Mission in Life.* Berkeley, CA: Ten Speed Press, 2000.

Buechner, Frederick. *Listening to Your Life.* San Francisco, CA: HarperSanFrancisco, 1992.

Buechner, Frederick. *Wishful Thinking: A Seeker's ABC.* San Francisco, CA: HarperSanFrancisco, 1993.

Canfield, Jack, and Mark Victor Hansen. *The Aladdin Factor.* New York, NY: Berkley Books, 1995.

Chapman, Annie, with Maureen Rank. *Smart Women Keep It Simple: Getting Free from the Unending Demands and Expectations on a Woman's Life.* Minneapolis, MN: Bethany House Publishers, 1992.

Cloud, Henry, and John Townsend. *12 "Christian" Beliefs That Can Drive You Crazy: Relief from False Assumptions.* Grand Rapids, MI: Zondervan Publishing House, 1995.

Guinness, Os. *The Call: Finding and Fulfilling the Central Purpose of Your Life.* Nashville: Word Publishing, 1998.

Jones, Laurie Beth. *The Path: Creating Your Mission Statement for Work and for Life.* New York, NY: Hyperion, 1996.

Lucado, Max. *Traveling Light.* Nashville: Word Publishing Group, 2001.

Miller, Arthur F. *The Power of Uniqueness.* Grand Rapids, MI: Zondervan, 1999.

Ortberg, John. *If You Want to Walk on Water, You've Got to Get Out of the Boat.* Grand Rapids, MI: Zondervan, 2001.

Palmer, Parker. *Let Your Life Speak.* San Francisco, CA: Jossey-Bass, 2000.

Ryan, M.J. *Attitudes of Gratitude: How to Give and Receive Joy Every Day of Your Life.* Berkeley, CA: Conari Press, 1999.

Shaw, Lynn. *Tee Hee Moments: Remembering to Laugh When You're Having One of Those Days!* Lebanon, IN: Affirmations Ink Press, 1999.

Smalley, Gary, and John Trent. *The Two Sides of Love.* Colorado Springs, CO: Focus on the Family Publishers, 1999.

Southard, Betty, and Marita Littauer. *Come as You Are: How Your Personality Shapes Your Relationship with God.* Minneapolis, MN: Bethany House Publishers, 1999.

Wildenberg, Lori, and Becky Danielson. *Empowered Parents: Putting Faith First.* Gainsville, FL: Synergy Publishers, 2003.

Willard, Dallas. *The Divine Conspiracy: Rediscovering Our Hidden Life in God.* San Francisco, CA: HarperSanFrancisco, 1998.

For More Information

Robin offers her program "Empowered with Purpose: Discovering Your Divine Assignment" in a retreat or seminar format. She also consults with groups and individuals and can even coach you through the process by phone. For more information on this and all of Robin's topics, products, and services, please visit her website at:

www.wisdomtreeresources.com
or email her at
yourwisdomtree@aol.com.

More Great Books from Harvest House Publishers

10-MINUTE TIME OUTS FOR MOMS
Grace Fox

This gathering of insightful devotions from author and mother Grace Fox encourages you to communicate with God throughout your day. Grace's homespun stories and Scripture-based prayers provide inspiration and practical guidance to help you maintain a vital connection with God. You'll discover refreshment and comfort as you spend each time-out with God.

30 DAYS THROUGH THE BIBLE
F. LaGard Smith

Noted *Daily Bible* author LaGard Smith takes you on a life-changing, 30-day devotional journey through God's Word. Insightful reflections coupled with highly significant Scripture passages explore the Bible's relevance for contemporary living. You'll discover an unfolding picture of the Bible's whole story, a comprehensive look at how the pieces of Scripture fit together, and an overview of the historical connections in the Bible.

THE REMARKABLE WOMEN OF THE BIBLE
Elizabeth George

Stories about Eve, Deborah, Sarah, Ruth, Mary, and other women from Scripture offer testimonies of changed lives and reflections on the remarkable strengths God cultivates in women who love Him. Conveying the assurance of God's love, Bible teacher Elizabeth George helps you connect with the source of fulfillment that sustained the women of the Bible—a relationship with God.

RADICALLY OBEDIENT, RADICALLY BLESSED
Lysa TerKeurst

Lysa TerKeurst shares illustrations from her life along with inspiring, biblical insights as she describes what it means to be totally, unapologetically obedient to Christ. You'll discover how to discern the voice of God and truly heed His call, see what radical obedience looks like on a daily basis, and catch the vision of Christ and make it your own. *Radically Obedient, Radically Blessed* is an invitation to seek God and boldly ask for and expect more from the Christian life.

WHEN GOD PURSUES A WOMAN'S HEART
Cindi McMenamin

Within the heart of every woman is the desire to be pursued, cherished, and loved. *When God Pursues a Woman's Heart* invites you on a personal journey of discovery that looks at the many ways God loves you, and how He shows that love. You'll come to know God as a Father who cares and understands, an encouraging Friend who cheers you on, a Comforter who is patient and compassionate, a valiant Knight who always comes to the rescue, and a Faithful One who will never leave. You'll gain greater confidence in your purpose in life as you see how much God longs to sweep you off your feet and love you as only He can.

JUST ENOUGH LIGHT FOR THE STEP I'M ON
Stormie Omartian

In a collection of devotional readings perfect for the pressures of today's world, Stormie Omartian helps you follow God in simple faith and eases your anxieties about the future. "More and more, God is teaching me to trust Him for every step I take...even when I can't see where I'm going," writes Stormie. This book of candid, poetic meditations reflects on the universal challenge of moving into uncharted waters when God has not given a clear picture of the destination.